How Fair the Meadows Are Today

Orville Taylor Bailey at home.

How Fair the Meadows Are Today

∽

PRESENTATIONS AT
THE CHICAGO LITERARY CLUB

by

Orville T. Bailey, M.D.

FONTIS PRESS
Westborough, Massachusetts

Library of Congress Control Number: 2001096346
ISBN 0–9711705–0–9
Printed in the United States of America.

The photographs in Chapter Nine were taken by and are the property of David R. Vopatek, with the exception of those otherwise attributed in their captions. The images in the preface are from Bailey family archives, with the exception of that on page xiv, a photograph taken by David R. Vopatek. The frontis is also a photograph by David R. Vopatek.

This book was designed by Janis Owens of Books By Design and typeset in 11.5/16 Minion by NK Graphics in Keene, New Hampshire. It was printed on Weyerhaeuser Cougar White by Thames Printing Company in Norwich, Connecticut, and bound in Skivertex by Acme Bookbinding Company in Charlestown, Massachusetts.

Do noble things, not dream them, all day long,
And so make life, and death, and that For Ever
One grand sweet song.

CHARLES KINGSLEY
A Farewell

The enclosed book is a collection of writings by Dr. Orville T. Bailey, delivered as oral presentations before members of the Chicago Literary Club over a period of some thirty years. It is being sent to members of the Chicago Literary Club and the Harvard Society of Fellows, as well as to other friends and colleagues. For more information, please contact David R. Vopatek at 2819 North Pine Grove Avenue, Chicago, IL 60657, or by telephone at (773) 348-7100.

Contents

〜

Foreword

Since the occasion is no secret, I can divulge that the date of Orville Bailey's birth was May 28, 1909. William Howard Taft was president, but the first decade of this century has other claims to fame and takes its wider cultural inspiration from the Edwardian Era. It was a time of international peace and of great talent in literature, music, and painting, looking to a new age of conspicuous consumption, of stunning fashions, and of Women's Lib, phase 1.

Orville's career, to simplify a lot, is a tale of five cities, one town, and one certified village. The cities are Syracuse, Albany, Boston, Indianapolis, and Chicago. The town is Cambridge, England. The village is Jewett, Greene County, New York, Orville's birthplace. Jewett, population then about 80, is in the upper Catskills. One is naturally reminded of Rip Van Winkle, who went up there to shoot squirrels, met some of the natives, got royally drunk on Holland gin, went into a deep slumber and didn't come down for 20 years. Orville clearly employed his time rather differently. He came down from the mountains at 15 years and enrolled at Syracuse University. At 19 he entered medical school at Union University in Albany, N.Y., graduating M.D. in 1932.

The text of this foreword is an address by Dr. Hubert R. Catchpole welcoming friends, colleagues, and students of Dr. Orville T. Bailey to a party in honor of his 80th birthday at the University Club of Chicago.

In a retrospective article appearing in *Journal of the American Medical Association* in November 1988, Orville detailed the history of neuropathology from its virtual inception, in 1930, to the present. He noted that the evolution of this field, and its extension and blossoming as a separate specialty, occurred during his own presence in it. Somehow he managed to avoid any suggestion of cause and effect. But in a more than 50-year career, centers of excellence in neuropathology simply had a habit of following Orville around.

Some highlights were Orville's war years in the remarkable team of Edwin Cohn at Harvard which separated blood cells and protein fractions for use in transfusions and developed fibrin foam as a hemostatic agent in neurosurgery, both invaluable militarily and scientifically as biochemical breakthroughs. Right after the war came a highly merited Guggenheim Fellowship at Cambridge and friendship with Adrian and Barcroft, giants of physiology. Then came involvement in the federal scientific expansion, the NIH study sections, and later the international community of neuropathology. In the sixties there was the publication with David Smith of *Experimental Models of Neurological Disease,* a coming of age of the discipline, and in the seventies service with the Space Science Board and, then and later, the honors proper to an elder statesman in neurological science. And always — perhaps this should have come first in terms of time and effort — service and the training of residents.

I have spoken rather narrowly of neuropathology. We also celebrate Orville as a master of conversation and of the written word; connoisseur of food and wine; opera buff; authority on crime, punishment, and the detective novel; expert on flowers and their close relatives, the weeds; and solver of the devilish Country Life crossword puzzles, where the clues are even more mysterious than the answers. A whole lot of this accumulated wisdom seems to derive from the early years in Jewett, New York, justifying the observation of Plutarch that an individual's achievements are a reflection of character, birth, and education. We salute an Edwardian gentleman.

Dr. Hubert R. Catchpole
Chicago, 1989

Preface

In his foreword, Hubert Catchpole suggests a connection between Orville Bailey's early life in Jewett, New York, and his subsequent interests and achievements. Here I shall explore this astute insight in the context of the immediate Bailey family, the community of Jewett at that time, and the natural attributes of this corner of the Catskill Mountains.

The Town of Jewett was a remote place in the early part of the twentieth century, a small world hemmed in by forested mountain ranges. Situated on a plateau at an elevation of more than 2,000 feet above sea level, it offered the freshest of air, sweet water from mountain springs, and brutally cold winters that often seemed interminable. The main occupation was dairy farming, with fields, orchards, and pastures wrested from hillsides. Few of the roads were paved, and stone walls lined the roadsides and divided fields one from another — products of the annual ascension of rocks from the thin subsoil.

The hard-working, no-nonsense inhabitants were, nonetheless, devoted to their grudging land. They worked variously at tending their animals, cutting hay from the uneven fields, planting and tending such crops as would mature in the brief summer, cutting wood in the fall, and "maple sugaring" in the spring. Wood was the fuel of choice, and each farmhouse had at least two woodstoves — one in

*A view of Cave Mountain, Jewett, New York. The Mountain Side House farm,
birthplace and childhood home of Orville Bailey, was situated on the shoulder of
the mountain, at left.*

the kitchen and one in the living area. The Presbyterian Church at
Jewett Heights was well-attended on Sunday mornings, and "social-
izing" for the most part involved visiting one's neighbors, all of
whom were known to everyone. Children were expected at an early
age to help with the various chores and farm work. Had Orville been
born into most families then, he might well have been forced into the
standard farm-boy mold, with no opportunity for his genius to develop — a nightmarish prospect in retrospect but one perfectly in
keeping with circumstances at that time.

Jewett Heights in the 1920s.

The Bailey family had established a presence in Jewett early in the nineteenth century, and the name of Orville's grandfather can be found on an 1867 map of the town. When he died, he left his farm to Orville's father, Milton O. Bailey, who married Ollie Persons from the nearby town of Lexington. Milton Bailey, standing well over six feet tall and broadly built, was a strongman in his time. He eventually became active in Greene County politics and was elected sheriff, serving in the post for many years. Although work on the land was turned over to a farmer who lived on the property, the Baileys continued to run the resort facility, called Mountain Side House. Such places were the summer haven of people from New York City. In those days, a man would bring his family to the country for the sum-

Milton O. Bailey's Mountain Side House.

mer, returning on weekends and for his vacation. The atmosphere was that of a large, extended family, with many people returning year after year. Days were spent observing farm work, hiking in the woods, and taking trips to nearby towns and scenic spots.

The young Orville — called "O.T." after his grandfather, a sobriquet used by those close to him throughout his life — no doubt found the city guests a stimulating presence, with new faces, different topics of conversation, and a glimpse of life beyond the mountains — a welcome relief from the isolation and loneliness of the long winter. He did not take to farm work, which no doubt disappointed his father but troubled his mother not at all. With her intercession, the young boy was given ample time to read and wander in the woods, no doubt observing and especially enjoying the rejuvenation of the countryside after the long winter. Indeed, in these pages he quotes from the third act of Parsifal to note "the resurgence of

Cows in the "fair meadows" of Mountain Side farm.

nature from its winter sleep [that] has from time immemorial stirred the deepest emotions of the human race."

Seventy years later he remembered springtime in the Catskills vividly, including the rare spots where spring beauties appeared at the margin of snow and icy water and where purple and painted trillium bloomed in the hemlock woods. It is reasonable to assume that his solitude in the midst of such natural beauty encouraged him to turn toward nature and stimulated his appreciation of its bounty in the fields and woods around the farm. Even years after he left home to pursue higher education, he occasionally returned to wander the mountaintop area, as evidenced in a letter to his cousin Hazel in 1938, with the return address of Dunster House C-44 at Harvard University: "This is just a note to go along with the prints of the pictures we

*Photographs taken by
O.T. Bailey during the
summer of 1938.*

took around Jewett this summer. We must take some more next year." Two of these prints are reproduced here. Their subject is an old stone chimney, probably part of a bygone maple sugaring structure, leaning away from the relentless winds of winter. True to character, he admired the aesthetics of the old chimney from a distance, but then came close to record the details of construction, stone on stone — artist and scientist, hand in hand. His letter goes on to say:

> I am particularly busy but enjoy my work. Mornings I am in Cambridge doing chemistry and mathematics; afternoons I am at the medical school carrying on some research. . . . I am still at Boswell's *Johnson* and probably will be for some time. . . . I have also read Professor Haskins' interesting book, *The Renaissance in the Twelfth Century.*

Although both his parents undoubtedly recognized their son's unusual intellect early on, his mother seemed particularly aware of his great potential, and it was she who nurtured his prodigious capacity to learn from the beginning. He played the piano well, and always acceded to his mother's request to perform a selection for visitors. She took great pride in all his accomplishments as long as she lived.

There was a one-room schoolhouse at Jewett Heights, which Orville attended several years until his older cousin, Hazel Bailey, convinced all parties that the young scholar should go to the high school in the adjoining town of Windham, even though he was very young to do so. Orville later saw this a turning point in his life, and he was immensely grateful to Hazel for enabling it. The dark side of this move, however, was the beginning of a long period of social isolation for him, during which he was always much younger than his classmates and therefore not compatible with them. He graduated from high school at the young age of only 15, and in the fall began his college career at Syracuse University, where of course his fellow students were older by several years, and this pattern persisted through his training at Albany Medical School. Only when he arrived at Harvard and Boston was he finally able to bask in the warmth of fellowship and develop a satisfying social life, but the isolation he had earlier endured produced a profound and lasting effect on him.

As O.T. Bailey made his way in the outside world, his former schoolmates and neighbors came to appreciate and admire his many accomplishments. Every now and then his name would appear in one of the local newspapers. *The Catskill Examiner,* for example, ran a story about him on July 3, 1952, that began as follows:

> Dr. Orville T. Bailey, a native of Greene County, has won not only national but international recognition, and since his own modesty and that of his parents, Sheriff and Mrs. Milton Bailey, have discouraged publicity of any sort, it seems appropriate this newspaper should acquaint Dr. Bailey's fellow citizens with a few facts regarding his work and let us all share in the honor that comes to all of us when one of us does so well.

The article goes on to describe his recent work and to announce his departure for Europe, where he was to give a series of lectures. The idea that a boy from Jewett had progressed so far that he was able to lecture people in other countries was undeniably uplifting.

And so it seems fair to say that there were, indeed, connections between O.T. Bailey's early days and his later life, confirming the wisdom of Plutarch as quoted by Hubert Catchpole. His writings for presentation at the Chicago Literary Club, each of which constitutes a chapter in this book, hint at some of those connections. The chapters are divided into three sections in accordance with their subject matter. Part One, "Of Botanists and Botany," reflects his lifelong interest in plants and flowers and in those such as John and William Bartram who excelled in their nurture. Part Two, "Portraits of Villainy," reveals his fascination with crime and punishment and the characters of criminals. And Part Three, "The Harvard Society of Fellows," provides a personal perspective on one of the premier intellectual groups of the twentieth century. Each part opening displays a quotation chosen by the editor with the conviction that it would have pleased him. Modest and unassuming as he was, O.T. Bailey would probably be surprised to see his writings published as a book, yet they constitute a cohesive and interesting collection, happily reflecting thereby many characteristics of their author. For the readers — friends, colleagues, and members of the Chicago Literary Club and the Harvard Society of Fellows — these pages will be a pleasant reminder of the rare human being who achieved so magnificently in his lifetime and graced the lives of so many by his presence.

Eugene Richard Bailey
Westborough, Massachusetts
October 2001

PART ONE

Of Botanists and Botany

Who loves a garden still his Eden keeps,
Perennial pleasures plants, and wholesome harvests reaps.

AMOS BRONSON ALCOTT, TABLETS
(1868)

CHAPTER ONE

Migration and Transformation

LET US CONSIDER the weed. "A weed is a plant which is not wanted in the place where it is growing," states a classic definition. This implies that in another place the same plant may be wanted and then would not be called a weed. Such is indeed the case. By migration and transformation, the weed may become a cherished possession of man. Conversely, other influences transform useful plants into weeds which interfere with man's objectives.

The concept *weed* is purely anthropocentric. "What is there in this plant for me? Or for mankind?" To see how the concept *weed* arose, it is necessary to look back to prehistory. The food of earliest man came from both plants and animals, whereas that of most other animals was one or the other. Plants were especially useful when hunting was poor. Some he preferred to others, but the most desirable sorts might be at the end of a hazardous journey.

Just how primitive man discovered that the ones he liked best could be moved to a place near his cave or hut is lost in the mists of time. Somehow he did so, only to find that plants already in that

Read at The Chicago Literary Club on January 6, 1975.

place would crowd out the ones he wanted. Again by means we can only conjecture, he learned that removal of unwanted plants would promote the growth of those which were the source of his food. Thus did the concept *weed* arise, coincident with the start of plant cultivation. As soon as man found ways of dealing with plants not wanted in the place where they were growing, a new phase of his environmental control began, one as important to his welfare as the discovery of fire. It was to lead, on the one hand, to the horticulture and agriculture of the present day and, on the other, to devastation and changes in ecological balance.

At an extraordinarily early time, primitive man also started to move near his dwelling and protect from unwanted sorts those plants which pleased his eye but did not appeal to his stomach. The concept of beauty in nature does not depend on a highly developed civilization, but is an essential human urge dating from the beginning of man himself.

Coming to historic times, one can see that there is no useful distinction between weeds and wild flowers. No matter how beautiful, a plant which interferes with the orderly pattern of a pleasure garden or the productivity of a vegetable plot is a weed. The same plant in woods or roadsides may be admired and, since it does no harm to man's objectives, it is called a wild flower. But it is the same plant. Any attempt at distinction is artificial and creates an unnecessary stumbling block to understanding the world around us.

The weeds of the northeastern United States have a special interest. When the first explorers arrived, they met plants they had never seen before. They and their followers took these back to the Old World, some for food, like potatoes, tomatoes, corn, and peppers; others to enrich their flower gardens. In that respect North America is not unique, for every corner of the earth has made similar contributions. On all continents, plants from one place have been transported to another and sometimes have become so fully naturalized as to be indistinguishable from native flora. In Britain, for instance, there are many plants which defy the wisest botanists to decide whether they are native, or spread by way of the land-bridge, or carried thence by ship.

Of the North American weeds, there is some documentation of arrivals. It is scanty, to be sure, but far from non-existent. Therein lies their peculiar interest to the historical botanist. Ann Leighton, in her book *Early American Gardens; For Meate and Medicine,* has gathered the available seventeenth-century documents and has studied the herbals in use by the New England worthies of the time. She has also observed the plants growing around abandoned seventeenth-century houses and in the New England countryside. As the title of her book implies, the New Englanders gardened for food and for the herbs which were their only sources of medicine. Of her authorities, the one most relevant to this essay is a bill for seeds sent by Robert Hill of London "dwelling at the three Angells in lumbar street" to John Winthrop, Jr., of Boston on July 26, 1631. The importance of this seed list is that it tells us precisely when certain plants were introduced. Several of these plants liked the American climate all too well and now are among our most troublesome weeds.

It is also interesting to consider why the colonists thought they needed these plants. The best authorities, Miss Leighton points out, are the herbals known to be in use in New England at that time — described in John Parkinson's *Paradisi in Sole Paradisus Terrestris,* Culpeper's *The English Physician, or an Astrologico-Physical Discourse of the Vulgar Herbs of this Nation,* and Thomas Johnson's revision of Gerard's *The Herball or General Historie of Plants.* Before considering specific examples of imported weeds, it might be well to look at one

5

weed known to be a native. Despite the seventeenth-century documentation, the source of some of our weeds is no more certain than that of Britain's.

The skunk cabbage (*Spathyema foetida*) is certainly a native American weed. It is a plant of swamps and damp woods from southern Canada to Georgia and westward to Illinois and Iowa. Its dependence on a wet, shady environment keeps it from spreading to places suited to agriculture, but it grows vigorously where the terrain meets its requirements. Skunk cabbage flowers are formed underground in autumn and generate so much heat as they press upward in earliest spring that the snow or ice cover melts. It is the welcome harbinger of the new season. Yet it has a distinctly fetid odor, almost like that of carrion. This is advantageous to the plant because it attracts insects for pollination at a time when few are about. Man dislikes this odor and consigns skunk cabbage to the category of weeds for this one characteristic alone. Though a few English lovers of the curious have incorporated it in their bog gardens, skunk cabbage remains essentially a weed of northeastern United States.

While there are many other and more troublesome native weeds, most of those which plague our gardens are imports. A large number of plants found their way to the United States in the first half of the seventeenth century. Some came purely by chance, as "passengers" in packing materials of shipments from England and Europe; others were inadvertently included among seeds of vegetables and flowers. Such accidents happened repeatedly in different shipments, with the result that gardeners in the United States must now contend with several species of the same weed.

Among the most common is bindweed. There are on this side of the Atlantic at least three distinct species, of which the field bindweed (*Convolvulus arvensis*) is the most troublesome of all. This arrived as a "passenger" in shipments during the first half of the seventeenth century. Grievous pest that it was on the other side of the Atlantic, it thrived in the American climate even better and spread until the precise volume of Rickett can give its present distribution only as "throughout the United States." It flourishes in the gardens and on the roadsides of Illinois; it populates every vacant lot in the city of Chicago. Its vines entwine our hedges and eradication is virtually impossible. There was a man who was obsessive about the neatness of his garden and an especial foe of bindweed. Dig out the roots as he would, it returned. Now it so chanced that he added a swimming pool to the amenities of his garden. When excavation had reached six feet, the roots of bindweed were still going down. At that point, he abandoned hope of clearing his garden. A dreadful progeny from a few seeds in packing material three hundred years ago!

Of the imported weeds, tansy (*Tanacetum vulgare*) is a good example. Today it runs rampant on roadsides, fields, and wastelands in most of the United States, crowding out other more desired plants. Yet it achieved this status by migration, for it is a European plant. We know to some extent when and how it reached North America. Though there were undoubtedly other importations, the seed order of John Winthrop, Jr., which Robert Hill of London filled on July 26, 1631, included tansy seeds. These tansy seeds have indeed numerous offspring.

But why did Winthrop want this plant? We must turn to the herbals known in Boston at that time. Gerard found it good for the "stomache"; the root "an especial thing against the gout"; the seed a medicine for worms. Parkinson again attributed these virtues to tansy but thought it also helped weak kidneys. Culpeper, with his astrological bent, placed it under Venus. If bruised and applied to the navel, it stayed miscarriages. All these herbalists mention tansy as a flavoring for food, and English social history of the time agrees. That experienced diner-out, Samuel Pepys, fancied a tansy cake with his savory. Life without tansy would have been dull, if not dangerous, in the seventeenth century.

Yet in New England it grew faster and faster because the limiting factors of soil and climate which controlled it in England did not exist in the New World. Leighton is led to remark, "Considering the New England countryside today, it is wonderful to think of a time when anyone would need to buy tansy seeds for twopence to be sent to New England."

Of the 59 sorts of seeds in the Winthrop order, another which has become a common weed is chicory (*Cichorium intybus*). It grows as a scraggly plant to five feet tall. From June to October it blooms in fields and roadsides almost everywhere in the United States. The vacant lots of Chicago are full of chicory. Yet the blue flowers scattered along the stems are beautiful in detail. Like tansy, all this chicory is descended from Winthrop's and other seventeenth-century New England gardens. Chicory is a rather attractive addition to the American landscape, even if generally unwanted. And all this from a penny-half penny worth of seeds.

Once again, we ask what Winthrop and the other Boston worthies wanted of this plant. Both Gerard and Culpeper regard chicory as "both binding and cleansing for the bowels; it helps a hot liver and jaundice; it prevents the stone and helps inflamed eyes." Parkinson also proposes the use of chicory as a salad and recognizes the bitterness of the root, which he thought could be removed by burying it in sand. The only modern use of this plant, on the contrary, depends on the preservation of this bitterness in the coffee of France, New Orleans, and the homes of a few gourmets. Witloof chicory, or endive, which we use for salads is quite a different plant (*Cichorium endivia*).

In the Winthrop list of 1631, we find "1 li carrett seed 12d per li." This would be the European species of carrot (*Daucus carota*), distinct from the Asiatic species from which the carrot of our vegetable gardens is derived. None of the herbalists had much use for the garden carrot, but Gerard and Culpeper found splendid virtues in the wild species. Gerard stated the plant was "windie" but the seed "consumeth windinesse and provoketh urine" and Parkinson agreed, though holding it in low esteem. Culpeper placed it under Mercury, wherefor it would "expel wind, remove stitches in the sides, provoke urine and womens' courses and remove the stone." If boiled in wine, "it helpeth conception."

Since the carrot seed is small, a pound would plant a very large area. This must have been the objective, for 12 pence was a considerable sum of money for the colonists in 1631. Inflation between that date and 1975 is at least 500 times and probably more. A pound of vegetable carrot seed now costs $9.86, which is much less in current values than Winthrop's 12 pence.

In the New World, the growing conditions so favored the European carrot that it spread to roadsides and waste places throughout North America. In the United States this weed is now called Queen Anne's lace, but it is quite different from the plant of that name in England — the cow parsley, *Anthriscus sylvestris*.

Winthrop's garden could hardly have been a colorful place. Modern reconstructions from existing records show that such gardens had an untidy charm. They were based on the English cottage gardens of the English villages at the time when the colonists emigrated. This form has had a singular persistence among the descendants of the settlers. I well remember from my boyhood similar gardens in upland Catskill farms, though the plants in them were ornamentals. Vegetables had been banished to a distant plot where they could be cultivated in rows, but it was the traditional cottage garden which was thought an appropriate setting for the farmhouse.

Some plants not on the Winthrop list were imported in the first half of the seventeenth century with equally great expectations, only to become weeds. Though records are silent as to who and when, the weeds are still with us in force. Pride of place in this group probably belongs to the dandelion (*Taraxacum* sp.). Since there are several species in the United States so similar that only a skilled botanist can tell them apart, there were almost certainly many separate importations. They now infest lawns all over the United States, especially the commonest variety, *Taraxacum officinale.*

One marvels today at the reasoning that led to this importation. Gerard thought that it cleansed and opened the bowels, strengthened a weak stomach, and helped the dysentery, incontinence, bladder troubles, and yellow jaundice. Culpeper put the dandelion in the dominion of Venus and in addition to Gerard's uses found it brought rest and sleep to those afflicted with "ague fits." He also mentioned that the French and Dutch ate dandelions in the spring, as do some people still, the only remains of this lore. To look at the lawns in Chicago, it is hard to realize that the dandelion is not a native plant, but the evidence that all species are migrants from the Old World is definitive.

Another plant which has been so prominent in the American landscape as to seem inevitably a native is the one called (in the United States) the daisy. It is, in fact, a wild chrysanthemum (*Chrysanthemum leucanthemum*). Although it interferes with hay meadows and garden crops in practically all of the United States, there is no denying its beauty.

However, the importations in the seventeenth century were for medical uses. Gerard found it valuable in "vulnerarie drinks," for treatment of gout and of inflammations of the eyes. It is just possible that some colonists craved the beauty of the daisy, which they had known at home. At any rate, this plant grew so well across the Atlantic that within a hundred years the daisy was accepted as a native plant in the meadows around Philadelphia, where John Bartram's life was so dramatically changed by "espying" one.

The plant we call a daisy is entirely different from the English daisy (*Bellis perennis*) in appearance, botanical structure, and growth requirements. The English daisy is a much smaller weed in English lawns when they receive less than meticulous care. It does not flourish in our cold winters, burning summers, and periods of drought. There were surely as many chances for it to arrive as a "passenger" as bindweed, but it has not survived in the eastern and central parts of the United States. The climate of San Francisco is more like that of England, and I was interested to note that the lawns in Golden Gate Park are as disfigured by English daisies as the worst tended lawn in England.

In all the examples cited so far, migration has transformed a useful plant into a weed. It is time to look at American plants which migrated from the New World to the Old, where the climate restrained their growth and where their beauty and novelty won them a place in gardens. The search for such plants is the basis for the great botanical expeditions sent out to many parts of the world over several centuries.

We might begin with beebalm, or as it is sometimes called, Oswego tea (*Monarda didyma*). This grows as a not very invasive weed in woods from New York to Michigan and south to Georgia and Tennessee. As the names imply, it was thought to be soothing to bee stings, and the leaves could be made into tisanes. Beebalm became a fixture of English herbaceous borders. There are now cultivars, but these differ little from the original species. After beebalm had received the approval of England, it was less scorned as an American garden subject but still is not as widely grown here as its brilliant flowers, hardiness, and disease resistance warrant.

One of the perennial jokes of Americans unlearned in botany concerns Englishmen who tend weeds in their gardens, one being goldenrod (*Solidago* sp.). There could hardly be a more familiar weed of meadows, hay fields, and roadsides from Canada to Tennessee and even Florida. Of the many wild species, the tall goldenrod (*Solidago gigantea*) is representative. There is one European species, called "woundwort" because it was thought to promote healing of wounds, but it was the American species which caught the fancy of the English gardeners. Gerard tells how fantastic prices were paid for the American goldenrod, only to collapse to nothing when a similar plant was found growing at the gates of London. Americans hate goldenrod because they think it is a great cause of hay fever. This attitude is largely unwarranted because most hay fever attributed to it results from the inconspicuous ragweed, which puts out its pollen at the same time that the striking flowers of the goldenrod appear nearby.

Not subjected to this delusion, even the most discriminating English gardeners admit the goldenrod to their herbaceous plantings and value its brilliant yellow flowers at a time when most other plants are not at their best. Thus has a weed been transformed into a garden plant by migration in space and liberation from bad company.

A remarkable example of the change in status of a plant by migration is the bitterroot (*Lewisia* sp.). The Lewis and Clark Expedition found it growing in uncounted myriads in and east of the northern Rockies. While many plants collected on that expedition were lost, the bitterroot arrived safely and was named *Lewisia* in honor of the leader of the expedition. Originating in one of the harshest climates the United States has to offer, it was admired by English gardeners but proved not to tolerate well the gentle climate of that country. Determined English connoisseurs then and now cosset this plant born in fierce snows and burning summers. A good specimen in an English rock garden is a triumph, and a fine example is sure of a prize in a Royal Horticultural Society show.

There is a familiar plant which illustrates all three attitudes toward botanical subjects — weed, wild flower, and garden plant — depending on the place where it grows. This is the mountain laurel (*Kalmia latifolia*), a native of the eastern United States, where it forms an evergreen shrub, usually as undergrowth in woods but also in more sunny locations if the soil is acid. Its beauty is generally admired in such places but it has been used only to a limited extent in the gardens of New England and other places with suitable climate and soil, perhaps because it is so easy to see in the wild.

The mountain laurel once played a role in American history, for Washington's soldiers made their beds from its leaves in the dreadful winter of 1777–1778 at Valley Forge, giving them such little comfort as they had. Mountain laurel still forms most of the undergrowth at Valley Forge. To see it in full bloom is to experience beauty mixed with poignancy and a sense of history. But this plant can become a weed in New England pastures and fields for years neglected, as they sometimes are. Then it provides a magnificent spectacle when in bloom. It shelters birds but bears mute testimony to hopeless agriculture.

When the mountain laurel was sent to Europe by Peter Kalm in the eighteenth century, it proved desirable for gardens but offered a challenge to gardeners. It is not quite so difficult in England as bitterroot, but a fine specimen is widely recognized as a token of a good gardener. Such are the many guises of the same plant, depending on whether or not it is wanted *in the place where it is growing.*

Fashion may also determine attitudes toward plants. To become a staple of the garden, a plant must appeal to many generations of gardeners. If it does not, it disappears. Take, for example our native stoneroot, *Collinsonia canadensis.* It is a plant of wet woods from Vermont to Wisconsin and south to Florida and Arkansas. To us it seems just another woodland plant and not a particularly attractive one at that. When John Bartram of Philadelphia sent seeds of stoneroot to his friend, Peter Collinson, in the 1740s, the reception was so enthusiastic that Collinson requested — even demanded — more shipments to satisfy the gardeners who wished to be in fashion.

At this distance, it is hard to see what the furor was about. Perhaps it was the curious form of the florets in an age when novelty in the garden, as elsewhere, was supreme. Stoneroot became a fad and passed like other fads, almost as quickly as "streaking." It has long since left the roster of English garden flowers.

We have considered wild plants which became garden subjects purely by migration in place without other transformation. There are other wild plants which have been so transformed by selection, propagation of sports, and hybridization that the humble plant of origin is difficult to visualize. One of these is the hardy American aster. Many species — all closely related — inhabit fields, meadows, and roadsides from southern Canada to Georgia and occasionally farther south, westward to Missouri, and north to British Columbia. The New England aster, *Aster novae-angliae,* may serve as an example. It flowers at much the same time as goldenrod, and the contrast of yellow and purple adds to the beauty of the countryside over large portions of the eastern United States.

Several of these American aster species found their way to

England and Europe, where hybridizers altered them until any relation to the wild plants is not easy to discern. They even acquired a new name, Michaelmas daisies. Today the autumn flower borders all over England are ablaze with the hybrids — white and pink, blue and purple in great masses.

When the Michaelmas daisies made the return trip across the Atlantic, they did not take kindly to the climate from which they sprung, and they are grown here only to a limited extent. As so often happens, selection was for large, varied flowers and tall plants at the expense of hardiness and drought tolerance, characteristics of less importance in English gardens than in our own. Thus did transformation of a plant by the hand of man progress so far that the plant could ill flourish in the place which gave it birth.

But the plant above all others that has been transformed by man is the rose. Nature provided species of roses in China and the Middle East and on the shores of the Mediterranean. From long before the dawn of history, these roses were valued beyond other plants, though to modern eyes the species forms are no more striking than many others and have the disadvantage of thorns.

When America was discovered thousands of years later, several rose species were found among its flora. A representative example is the pasture rose, *Rosa virginiana.* Included in its distribution are the upland pastures of the Catskills, where I have seen it growing as a weed, its thorns pulling on the hair of cattle and scratching the herdsman.

The rose of any species has a stronger tendency toward variation in nature than most other plants. It frequently puts out sports, that is, branches which are different from the rest of the plant. If cuttings are made from these sports, the resulting plants resemble the sport and not the parent. One such variation is doubling, the occurrence of two or more rows of petals instead of one, as usual in the species. For some reason, the double forms have been especially esteemed from the earliest days of horticulture.

In historic times, the Romans valued the rose above all other flowers, and masses appeared at their banquets. It is not certain that the plant called "rose" by the Romans was limited to the one we now call by that name. Their writings state that roses were brought from Egypt across the Mediterranean to Rome, then a voyage of many days or weeks. The plant we know as "rose" could not withstand such treatment in that climate without refrigeration. Whatever it was, some sort of plant called rose was synonymous with beauty and luxury to the Romans.

By the Middle Ages we are on safer grounds. Recognizable roses appeared in paintings and occasionally in sculpture. The position of this plant as the most beautiful of all was unchallenged. It shared with the Madonna lily the distinction of being a symbol of the Virgin Mother of God. When She is shown in a rose garden, we learn how medieval roses were grown. It was at this time that there began the custom of bestowing a rose fashioned in gold on monarchs or institutions in recognition of services to the Church as the mark of the Pontiff's greatest favor. For a thousand years this custom has continued. The present Pope presented a golden rose to the Church at Bethlehem in the 1960s.

Throughout their history, the Persians have had a veritable passion for roses. Roses appear everywhere in their art. As early as the eleventh century Omar Khayyam wrote:

> *Why dost thou sell the rose for silver,*
> *For what more precious than the rose canst buy?*

(Even though Fitzgerald's translation changes the lines to praise of wine.)

In the seventeenth century, there arose a great school of flower painting in Holland and Flanders. The artists included many roses in their pictures, fully double blooms with rather loose petals. The dominance of the rose is suggested by the arrangement of their bouquets — roses front and center. By this time there were many forms from which to select. Their paintings teach us what varieties were most admired at that time.

These painters were almost contemporary with our herbalists. So prominent a flower as the rose merited their deepest speculations. Parkinson grew 24 varieties in his garden. He records the rose's "sweet water" as useful in "binding and loosening" while its perfume in "sweet bags" caused "solubleness." Gerard's long list may be summed up by saying that the rose soothed almost any pain — ulcers, old wounds, weak eyes — and strengthened the heart, liver, and kidneys. Culpeper put red roses under Jupiter, damask under Venus, and white under the moon. His uses accord with those of Gerard and Parkinson. Rose water was a frequent flavoring for pastries and sauces. A few nostalgic gourmets use it thus at the present time, but such a taste is rare.

The twentieth century has seen one scientifically valid use of the rose in preventive medicine. Seed pods of roses are large, firm structures in all varieties and in some are so prominent and brightly colored as to be a chief beauty of the plant; they are called "rose hips." At the outbreak of World War II it had been known for some time that rose hips are one of the richest sources of vitamin C, having eight times the content of orange juice. Importations of conventional sources of this vitamin into Britain were severely curtailed and chemical plants could not be spared to manufacture it synthetically, so volunteers all over Britain gathered the hips from the thousands of roses in its gardens. These were made into a syrup which saved British children from scurvy through those dark years.

To return to the seventeenth century, Governor Bradford recorded roses growing in Plimouth Plantation. Despite the herbalists, these were probably chiefly for beauty. It tells much about the Massachusetts colonists that the first things they wanted after basic necessities were a university and roses.

The rose as ideal beauty is celebrated in the literature of all times. Until the non-objectivists, every great painter has depicted roses at some stage of his career. Music, too, has celebrated the rose. Some of the finest *Lieder* concern roses, and they appear in opera — for instance, Richard Strauss's *Der Rosenkavalier*. There the plot is based on a genuine custom in eighteenth-century Vienna, whereby a nobleman wishing to make a proposal of marriage sent an emissary bearing a silver rose to the lady of his choice. Stage designers have used their utmost skill on the rose to be presented by Octavian to Sophie in Act II.

By the early eighteenth century, the number of rose varieties had become very large. These, it must be recalled, had all resulted from chance crosses or from selective cultivation of nature's experiments in the form of sports. In the second half of that century, botanists discovered how to make intentional crosses, the progeny hopefully having the best characteristics of each parent. The American and Chinese species, too, then became available in Europe. Results were accelerated by the knowledge of heredity which the nineteenth century brought. So great became the selection that the most popular kinds at any period are a reliable index of taste at that time and place.

In the Napoleonic era, the Empress Josephine wanted to grow every sort of rose in the world in her gardens at Malmaison. It was said that the most certain way for a general to curry favor with Napoleon was to bring back a new rose for the Empress. She commissioned the great flower painter, Redouté, to record them and the result is one of the finest series of botanical paintings ever made. The delicacy, grace, and refinement of the roses Redouté painted perfectly reflect the taste of Josephine and her court.

The Victorian age preferred roses which were solid, even ponderous. They had a compact infolded form and garish colors and seem to us a bit stodgy. (There could be worse characterizations of the ruling classes in the days of that great queen!) Present-day taste favors the high centered form. It has the austere elegance of a Mies van der Rohe building. Such a rose holds within its genes contributions from at least three continents, crossed and recrossed times without number until all knowledge of its lineage is lost. There is as much botanical fact as poetry in the familiar lines of Walter de la Mare:

> *Oh, no man knows*
> *Through what wild centuries*
> *Roves back the rose.*

Disappointing though the rose may be as a medicinal herb, except under unusual circumstances, it has passed from humble weed to the ultimate examplar and symbol of beauty.

Some weeds have not disappointed either as medicine or as garden subjects. One is the foxglove (*Digitalis purpurea*), a wild plant of the English countryside, including Shropshire and neighboring counties. In the hands of skilled hybridizers it has acquired new colors and changed markings. They also have become tall, imposing plants. While these foxgloves brighten the summer garden, they have to be used with care where children or animals are about because of the property which makes it feared — intensely poisonous leaves. This property has been known for centuries. Like most poisonous herbs, it found its way into the apothecary's brew and the secret formulae of witch doctors. Most of these plant mixtures now seem useless and are sometimes dangerous, but the foxglove is an exception.

Its introduction into scientific medicine by Dr. William Withering is a landmark in history of that art. Born in Shropshire, he doubtless knew the foxglove from childhood and perhaps admired it, for his illustration in his memoir, "An Account of the Foxglove," shows flower instead of the leaf, which contains the medically active principle. His account of his discovery in this book is worth quotation:

> In the year 1775 opinion was asked concerning a family recipe for the cure of dropsy. I was told that it had long been kept a secret by an old woman in Shropshire who had sometimes made cures after the more regular practitioners had failed. I was informed also that the effects produced were violent vomiting and purging; for the diuretic effects seemed to have been overlooked. This medicine was composed of twenty or more different herbs; but it was not very difficult for one conversant in these subjects to perceive that the active herb could be no other than foxglove.

But no one had ever understood before; such observations are made only by the talented few. It is now known that the principal effect is on the heart muscle rather than on the kidneys. Withering later became a successful Birmingham practitioner, treating such eminent patients as Benjamin Franklin, but his enduring fame rests on his studies of a Shropshire weed. As well it might, for the botanical name of the foxglove is *Digitalis*. The plant's way of making digitalis long eluded the synthetic chemists, but recently Woodward has synthesized one of the active substances. The process is difficult and expensive, and impractical commercially, and all the digitalis used in medicine today comes from the leaves of plants. Weed though it may be, it has prolonged or saved the lives of millions of people with heart disease.

Some weeds have given the necessary clues to chemists. An almost leafless shrub, 2 to 3 feet tall, grows near the seacoast of southern China. In appearance, it is not attractive even when it bears its small blossoms in summer. The Chinese call it Ma Huang and have used it as medicine for over 5,000 years, along with many other weeds and shrubs. To modern Western eyes, the rationale for the use of Ma Huang and other Chinese plants seems incomprehensible. Morse states, "The key to treatment is in the production or depletion of Yang and Yin in the body, or parts of the body, through the action of suitable remedies, and this secures equilibrium of the flow of these cosmic forces." Before making any remarks about this reasoning, it is well to inquire whether the Chinese philosophy is more obscure than Culpeper's astrological botany.

An active principle was isolated from Ma Huang in 1885, but Western medicine knew nothing of it until Chen of the Lilly Laboratories brought it here in 1923. Convinced that there was some basis for the strange tales, he worked out the physiological action and by 1928 had synthesized the active substance. This Chen called ephedrine, since the Western botanical name for Ma Huang is *Ephedra sinica*. All the ephedrine used in the United States is now made synthetically, but other countries still get most of their supply from the plant.

It was known that adrenalin gives immediate relief for many conditions due to allergy, including bronchial asthma. The improvement disappears as rapidly as it comes on. Ephedrine has a similar effect, but its action is slow and persists for some time. The two can therefore be used to supplement each other.

Is this weed substance, then, of any value? More than once I have watched a well-loved child, limp, blue, and gasping from asthma, instantly restored to normal color and breathing by an injection of adrenalin and maintained in that state by a substance in this obscure Chinese plant. Do not despise the weed.

And do not despise the weed in the human garden. It is true that mankind has its bindweeds, individuals whose contribution to the ultimate good of humanity is not immediately to be discerned. But there are others with much to offer who poorly fit the common mould at the place and time in which they find themselves. These, too, can become treasures of human society by migration in space but more significantly in time, for time is like a refiner's fire. Examples are numerous, perhaps as many as there are great steps forward in human progress. I cite only one.

Galileo Galilei was born in Pisa in 1564 but came to Florence by way of Padua. He discovered the mountains on our moon, the phases of Venus, the moons of Jupiter, and many stars in the Milky Way. All these observations and more made him an important figure in Italian intellectual circles. But his studies of sunspots led him to conclude that the sun rotates. This discovery convinced him that Copernicus had been right when he proposed a century earlier that the earth also rotates on its axis, producing day and night, and that the planets revolve about the sun. Copernicus escaped conflict because he delayed publication, the first copy of his book reaching him only on his deathbed. Galileo, however, made his pronouncement while in full vigor and at the height of his reputation. At once he attacked the existing scientific authorities with more energy than tact, and conflict with the Church was inevitable. In the life of his time, Galileo had been transformed into a weed which had to be rooted out before it overran the garden. This was attempted by the Inquisition with threat of torture. On the 22nd of June in 1633, he read his recantation and was incarcerated at the pleasure of the tribunal. There is a legend — nothing more — that after the recantation Galileo exclaimed, "But still it moves." Apocryphal as this probably is, it is consistent with his behavior for the remaining nine years of his life. Sure in his convictions, he lived quietly and continued his work on mechanics and astronomy until stopped by hopeless blindness. The efforts of the Inquisition contained the weed for a time but could not destroy it. Today we send men to the moon and space ships to distant planets in the sure and certain knowledge that the earth does indeed rotate and the planets do revolve about the sun. The seventeenth-century weed has been transformed into a benefactor of mankind, as have the aster, the rose, and the foxglove.

On another plane, there are those called eccentrics, amiable or otherwise. Weeds though they may be, they make their contributions to those who pause to understand. The Senior Common Rooms of Harvard and Oxford, the Combination Rooms of Cambridge — and, yes, the Chicago Literary Club — are places where they are respected and cherished. For some at the end there are Nobel Prizes and enduring fame. For many more, there lingers the fragrance of a rare personality and an enrichment of life.

Whether botanical or human, the weed can teach us much. From it we learn vigor and persistence and courage and the beauty which is ours for the seeing.

Do not despise the weed.

BIBLIOGRAPHY

Bloom, A. *Perennials for Your Garden.* Nottingham, England: Floraprint Ltd., n.d.

Carey, M.C., and D. Fitchew. *Wild Flowers at a Glance.* London: J.M. Dent and Sons, Ltd., 1961 (reprinted 1971).

Coats, P. *Flowers in History.* London: Weidenfeld and Nicolson, 1970.

Coats, P. *Roses: Pleasures and Treasures.* New York: G.P. Putnam's Sons, n.d.

House, H.D. *Wild Flowers of New York,* Memoir 15 (2 parts). State Museum of the State of New York, published by the State of New York, 1923.

Günthart, L. *The Glory of the Rose.* London: George G. Harrap Co., Ltd., 1965.

Kalm, P. *Travels into North America,* transl. J.R. Forster. Barre, Vermont: Imprint Society, 1972.

Leighton, A. *Early American Gardens,* "For Meate or Medicine." Boston, Mass: Houghton Mifflin Co., 1970.

Morse, W.R. *Chinese Medicine, Cleo Medica,* ed. E.B. Krumbhaar, 1934.

Paviere, S.H. *Floral Art: Great Masters of Flower Painting.* Leigh-on-Sea, England: F. Lewis, Publishers, Ltd., 1965.

Peck, T.W. and K.D. Wilkinson. *William Withering of Birmingham, M.D., F.R.S., F.L.S.* Baltimore, Md.: Williams and Wilkins Co., 1950.

Prentice, T.M., and E.O. Sargent. *Weeds and Wildflowers of Eastern North America.* Barre, Vermont: Peabody Museum of Salem and Barre Publishers, 1973.

Redouté, P.-J. *Roses.* New York: Ariel Press, British Book Centre, 1954.

Rickett, H.W. *Wild Flowers of the United States: Vol. I. The Northeastern States* (2 parts). New York: McGraw-Hill Book Co. (third printing, with revisions), 1973.

Roddis, L.H. *William Withering: The Introduction of Digitalis into Medical Practice.* New York: Paul B. Hoebar, Inc., 1936. (see esp. p. 50).

Shanks, P. (ed.) *The Golden Homes Encyclopedia of Garden Plants.* London: Marshall Cavendish, 1973.

Wilkinson, J.V.S., and L. Binyon. *The Shāh-Nāmah of Firdausi: The Book of the Persian Kings.* London: Oxford University Press, 1931.

CHAPTER TWO

Chance Favors
the Prepared Mind

⤳

NEVER GET INTO BIOGRAPHY, it throws too harsh a light on the prevalence of lunacy," says James Thurber. With respect, I disagree. History offers nothing more fascinating than the study of a person's progress through daily events, each ordinary in itself, to an achievement memorable enough to merit recall decades or centuries later. What strikes one repeatedly is that the final accomplishment is the result of interaction between a person in some way of exceptional capacity and external events which are unforseen and unforseeable. There is an aphorism of Pasteur, "All great discoveries are the result of chance, but chance favors the prepared mind." If the word *discoveries* is changed to *achievements,* the statement embraces all human accomplishment with fewer exceptions than there are to most generalizations. Let us examine a specific instance of this phenomenon.

On August third in 1803, a seventh son was born to William and Anne Paxton in Milton Bryant, Bedfordshire, a hamlet of thatched and gabled cottages set in green fields and noble trees. The boy they

Read at the Chicago Literary Club on February 13, 1978.

named Joseph was destined for a harsher childhood than even that expected among small farmer's families in early nineteenth-century England. The father died when Joseph was a small boy and his mother, too poor to raise so large a family, put him to be brought up by an elder brother. Here conditions were so severe that in later life he rarely spoke of them willingly, but on one occasion he said to his daughter, "You never know how much nourishment there is in a turnip until you have had to live on it." Poverty combined with sternness amounting to cruelty in the household led Joseph to run away. His wanderings led him to Essex, where a Quaker named Ford befriended him. In those days, an ambitious lad without education or patron could find few avenues of advancement except as a gardener, and he may have been encouraged by his Quaker friend, as among Quakers of the time gardens were not only a passion but also had a religious significance, as they regarded plant life as a manifestation of God's nature.

Somehow or other he was back in Bedfordshire by 1818, when he was 15, working as a garden boy at Battlesden Park. There he stayed two years, then went to Woodhall, and at 19 was back once more at Battlesden Park. But he was ambitious beyond these jobs, and the great city of London drew him like a magnet. The Horticultural Society (now the Royal Horticultural Society) had recently started Chiswick Gardens, with their new opportunities for study and advancement. To this institution Joseph was admitted in 1823, carefully adding two years to his real age of 20 as he did so. Promotion quickly followed to the responsible position of foreman. So far, the story could be that of hundreds of small farmer's sons, but now Chance seized this young man and changed his life for the first, but by no means for the last, time by bringing him and the sixth Duke of Devonshire together — the small farmer's son and the most noble of the English nobility, the master of Chatsworth, the greatest of great houses.

Since this meeting is so crucial to our story, it is well to view it in the words of Paxton's distinguished granddaughter, Violet Markham:

> The chance that two circles so remote should ever touch was of all hazards the greatest, let alone that having touched, one orbit should revolve round the other for the rest of their joint lives. . . . Yet Fate had written in her book that no two men should be bound together by ties of affection more intimate than those that were to unite the Duke of Devonshire and his gardener. . . .
>
> Before the advent of Paxton, the Duke was no gardener, as his own account of Chatsworth proves. But he came in touch, so to speak, by accident with horticulture. Lady Charlotte Boyle had brought to the Cavendishes by marriage the beautiful house at Chiswick which was the Duke's favourite residence — one he preferred, indeed, to the historic mansion in Piccadilly.
>
> A gate divided the Duke's garden from the grounds of the Horticultural Society. It was a pleasant stroll on a fine day from one to the other. Though not at that time an enthusiast, he found much to interest him in the Society's plants and flowers, for new varieties were very fashionable and the curious were interested in such things.
>
> During his strolls his attention was drawn to a short, pleasant-looking young man who often opened the gate for him. This, he was told, was the gardener in charge, primarily of creepers and new plants. Something about the young man's appearance and his general air of alertness struck the Duke. He talked to him

27

frequently, and found his intelligence quite out of the ordinary. So much so, that when the post of head gardener at Chatsworth fell vacant in the spring of 1826, the Duke came to a sudden and, in the circumstances, very surprising decision. He proposed to put a lad of twenty-three, earning as many shillings per week as he had years over his head, in charge of the Chatsworth Gardens.

Consider the multiplication of chances: that the Horticultural Society had established its garden at Chiswick, that Paxton had chosen this garden for further training, that Lady Boyle had married into the Duke's family, that the Duke did not much care for his great mansion in central London, that he used one particular gate on his walks. Lack of any one would have broken the chain. But Paxton's quickness in mastering the science and art of horticulture, his pleasant personality, and his ready conversation — these belong to the prepared mind.

The appointment was made on May 7, 1826. Two days later the Duke left for a diplomatic mission to Russia as the British representative to the coronation of Emperor Nicholas I. But Paxton, without losing a moment, set off for Derbyshire by coach, arriving at Chatsworth at 4:30 A.M. At once he explored the grounds and clambered over a wall to inspect the kitchen garden, finishing by 6 A.M., when he set the men to work and had the waterworks turned on. All this before time for breakfast with the housekeeper, Mrs. Gregory. It was an eventful meal, for Chance was again in full cry. By chance, Mrs. Gregory had as her guest her niece, Sarah Bown. Let the granddaughter tell what happened:

Fate met Paxton on the threshold of Chatsworth with a double shot in her locker. On the day of entering his new employer's service, he also met his future wife — the woman whose influence was to be paramount in his life. For thirty-two years he was to be swayed like a planet revolving round two stars. For each of these persons, his master and his wife, he had unbounded affection and loyalty. He was able to combine the utmost devotion for the Duke with devotion no less great for the woman he had married. If he owed to the Duke the opportunities of which he made full use, I have no hesitation in saying that without Sarah Bown, the housekeeper's niece with whom he fell in love at breakfast the first morning, the world would never have heard his name.

Not in the least overwhelmed by his double good fortune, Paxton at once put his uncontrollable energy to work in clearing up and improving the neglected — perhaps unloved — gardens of Chatsworth. Results came quickly. When the Duke returned from his diplomatic mission in Russia on December 9th, exactly seven months later, he wrote in his diary, "Arrived at Chatsworth de gioia, I am enchanted with the progress. My new gardener, too, Paxton has made a great change."

That Paxton was a skillful gardener had already been demonstrated at Chiswick, but Chatsworth gave him his first opportunity to organize, inspire, and direct the huge workforce so great a house had at its command. In October 1832, Princess Victoria, then in her fourteenth year, and her mother, the Duchess of Kent, with the inevitable Sir John Conroy, paid a visit to Chatsworth. To entertain the Heiress Presumptive, Paxton arranged the expected illuminations and other festivities in the garden, but one problem worried him. In a Derbyshire October, paths are likely to be littered with fallen leaves and hence untidy. Paxton kept a workforce of 100 men working through the night removing the leaves and rolling the walks. Victoria, even then observant, was puzzled by the neatness and was astonished at the pains used to achieve it. The resources at Paxton's disposal astonish us 150 years later as much as the tidiness did the Princess.

In Derbyshire, the climate is not favorable for tender plants and winters are colder than in many other parts of England. This led Paxton to consider improvements in greenhouse design. Those being used had heavy framework, which not only made them expensive but also cut down the light except at mid-day, when they admitted too much. Paxton's designs had light framework and the roofs slanted at an angle such that they caught the maximum amount of light when the sun was low and least when it was high. These principles have remained basic to greenhouse design ever since. They also put greenhouses within the reach of the general public. Today in England, even quite small gardens seldom lack a greenhouse, and they look very much like Paxton's published designs. In fact, some later gardeners, giving complete allegiance to the designs of Robinson and Gertrude Jekyll, have decried Paxton as the person responsible for making possible the "bedding-out" schemes of Victorian gardeners and of public parks to the present day. But Paxton should not be blamed if later gardeners have put his inventions to banal uses.

These designs were only preliminary to a plan on quite a different scale. One amenity which Chatsworth lacked was a conservatory on a scale worthy of the Duke of Devonshire. It is impossible to overemphasize the status value of a huge greenhouse or conservatory to a person of wealth and rank in the nineteenth century. Beside it, collections of books or paintings — even racing stables — paled into insignificance. To fill the vast structures, expeditions went to the warm countries of the world — China, India, Ceylon, Africa, South America — bringing back rare plants at the expense of great suffering and many lives. So the Duke of Devonshire would be expected to have the greatest conservatory of them all.

By 1837 Paxton was ready to proceed with the Great Conservatory, which was complete and planted by 1840. It was the largest glass building in the world: 277 feet long, 123 feet wide, and 67 feet at its highest point. There were central and side aisles covered by an ingenious and original curvilinear roof, the whole being filled with tropical plants. In the course of time, the Duke organized two plant-hunting expeditions of his own without much success. One of these plant hunters was Gibson, sent to Calcutta to obtain *Amherstia nobilis,* the fabled tree of Ind, whose blood-red flowers were offered as sacrifice to Buddha. Gibson brought back one plant safely but Paxton could not make it flower. There were, however, many other new plants in Gibson's shipments. The other expedition was to western North America. It ended abruptly and tragically when the two plant hunters were drowned at the mouth of the Columbia River, just as they were starting to collect. That is the kind of human misery and sacrifice that filled the great glass status symbols of the English nobility.

While the Great Conservatory was being built and planted, the Duke made the Grand Tour of the Continent for 18 months in 1838 and 1839. Despite Paxton's obligations at Chatsworth, the Duke insisted that he come along, leaving his wife Sarah to carry out the instructions that Paxton sent by letter. From then on, this was to be the pattern: Joseph making the overall plans and Sarah implementing them in their details.

It was a fortunate arrangement. Paxton buffered the Duke against the mischances of travel and the daily contact brought an even closer mutual trust and friendship, for their association had long since transcended the employer-employee relation. When the Duke's courier proved incompetent, Paxton quietly smoothed the obstacles, even cooking the Duke's dinner on one occasion when no proper cook could be found, to the Duke's pleasure and amazement. This intimate contact with a man of utmost education and position, combined with the travel experience, prepared Paxton to emerge onto a wider scene.

In the 1840s, this preparation and his gift for friendship brought him into contact with leading literary figures, and Charles Dickens became a close associate. He founded two journals, the *Horticultural Register* and *Magazine of Botany*. Much of the material he wrote himself in a clear, literate, informative style. His granddaughter records her surprise that a person of so meager an education could do this, giving as possible explanations the stimulus of his wife and the association with the Duke. But is it so amazing? Paxton's near contemporary, Abraham Lincoln, had even less education and little, if any, contact with people of learning, yet his mature style is admired throughout the English-speaking world and some European critics, not otherwise notably pro-American, have pronounced it the finest in the English language. But the grandeur of style in the Gettysburg Address and the Second Inaugural was not for Paxton. Style can be enhanced by education and especially by practice, but at base it is inborn.

The 1840s saw the rapid expansion of railroads until they dominated not only travel but finance. Paxton's gift for friendship carried him into the midst of it in that such leaders as George Stephenson knew and trusted him. Paxton carefully made use of these contacts to invest his modest savings in railroad stocks, Joseph indicating the direction and, as in the garden, Sarah watching the day-to-day fluctuations of the stock market. The result was that the Paxtons accumulated a very substantial fortune.

Meanwhile, the Duke of Devonshire was piling up debts on a scale so large that his solicitors could find no solution. It is true that Paxton's works were expensive. Besides the Great Conservatory, he had designed an arboretum on botanical principles, the Emperor Fountain with the highest jet in Europe, and the Great Rockery, then as now perhaps the greatest consumer of labor in gardening. But his was a minor contributor to the situation. The Duke's deafness made him more dependent on lavish entertainments at frequent intervals on a scale than even the Devonshire fortune could stand. For instance, there was the visit of the Queen and Prince Albert in December 1843, when the lack of horticultural display was compensated for by illuminations of waterfalls, cascades, fountains, and the Great Conservatory, all synchronized, no small feat without electricity. The Duke of Wellington, a member of the party, got up early to view the mess left by the revels but found every vestige removed. "I should have liked that man of yours for one of my generals," said the Victor of Waterloo to the Duke of Devonshire.

Paxton was as efficient about the debt as he was in clearing the garden. He presented to the solicitors a plan which they accepted — no small tribute to his integrity and judgement. It involved the sale of certain lands for which Paxton was able to get a high price because of his involvement in railroad affairs, choosing those which would yield an immediate profit for sale and retaining the long-term investments. Within a very short time the debt was discharged and the Devonshire fortune was intact. Chatsworth was also becoming a tourist attraction. Sixty thousand people visited it per year in this period.

As the 1840s drew to a close, Paxton, the gardener at heart, was to end them with a botanical triumph which was also the preparation for his crowning achievement. Frustrated in his attempt to get the sacred tree of Ind to flower, he set about in 1849 to grow the fantastic water lily *Victoria regia* (now changed to *Victoria amazonica*). Seen in various rivers in tropical South American rivers between 1801 and mid-century, viable seeds reached Kew only in 1846, being brought by Bridges. Sir Robert Schomburgk, finding it on New Year's Day in 1837 on the River Berbice, British Guiana, described it in this way:

> A gigantic leaf from five to six feet in diameter, salver shaped with a broad rim of a light green above and a vivid crimson below, was resting upon the water. Quite in character with the wonderful leaf was the luxuriant flower, consisting of many hundred petals passing in alternate tints from pure white to rose and pink — the ribs are very prominent — almost an inch high, radiating from a common center.

Since I have seen it growing, I can attest to the accuracy of this description. At Kew, the seeds germinated but grew poorly and did not flower.

In July 1849 Paxton persuaded his friend Sir William Hooker, Director of Kew, to let him have a plant. At 6 A.M. on August 3, 1849, Paxton himself took possession of the plant and carried it by train to Chatsworth, where a tank 12 feet square by 3 feet 4 inches deep awaited it. Conditions of temperature and lighting simulated those of the tropics, but most important was the use of a waterwheel to keep the water in gentle motion, as in the great rivers of its native habitat. By mid-September the size of the tank had to be doubled. On October 15, leaves were 4 feet 5 inches across, while the one at

Kew measured only 5 inches. On November 2, Paxton, in great excitement wrote the Duke at Lismore, his Irish estate, "Victoria has shown flower!! — No words can describe the grandeur and beauty of the plant."

This brought the Duke back in all haste to see the botanical marvel. The excitement was shared by the eponymous Queen, and on November 13 Paxton went to Windsor with a leaf and a fully opened blossom. No details of the presentation survive, but it must have had its comic side since the diameter of the leaf was greater than the height of Her diminutive Majesty.

Home again at Chatsworth, Paxton demonstrated the strength and power of flotation in the leaves by having his daughter Annie, aged 7, put on one leaf by the Duke and Lady Newberg. A charming engraving records the incident. A leaf could, in fact, sustain a weight of 100 pounds, while Annie then weighed only 70.

To enshrine this greatest of Paxton's botanical triumphs, he built a special Lily House at a cost of £800. The method of construction involved several novel features and the lessons provided by the remarkable ribs of the leaves were fully used. This conservatory had a ridge-and-furrow principle in its design; a roof that was also a light and heat adjuster; iron columns which were also drain pipes; rafters and sash bars that served the same purpose but were arranged to conserve moisture; and a floor which was not only a floor but also a ventilator and dust trap.

It was at this point that Paxton received his greatest gift from the Goddess of Chance. As the construction of the Lily House on novel principles was going forward, there was a stir in the air throughout Britain about a great exhibition to be held in London the next year. Queen Victoria repeatedly stated that it was "all the work of my beloved Angel," but this was not quite the case. The conception was basically that of Henry Cole, a civil servant trained in the law, who had turned his hand to publishing (including the world's first Christmas card), to china design, and to other artistic endeavors. He came to the attention of Prince Albert when the Prince was made president of the Royal Society of Arts. Albert was never content to be a figurehead, and he embraced causes, the first being an exhibition of art manufactures to be held in London in 1848. This was about to flounder for lack of exhibits when Cole personally visited manufacturers and obtained 20,000. Despite the fateful year, there were many foreigners among the 70,000 visitors. Three more exhibitions repeated the pattern in London and Birmingham.

The next year Cole visited the Paris Exhibition and came away with the idea that British manufacturers should face up to the international competition. It was only then that the suggestion of international scope appeared. Prince Albert was at first disquieted, but then turned Cole's view back to him as his own. The Prince became enthusiastic but felt the planned site, the courtyard of Somerset House, was too small, suggesting instead the level area in Hyde Park opposite Knightsbridge Barracks. As Bird comments, "This seemed as harmless as it was sensible, but in the light of slightly later events, the Prince might have stirred up less-trouble had he proposed turning Buckingham Palace into a brothel." Indeed, the hue-and-cry was terrific: The building would never be removed and Hyde Park thereby spoiled, a squatter would have to be displaced, and above all, a group of aging elms must be cut down — among other equally odd objections.

Nonetheless, a competition for plans was instituted and 245 were submitted, each more unsuitable than the other. Thereupon the building committee produced its own plan. It is well recognized that a camel is a horse designed by a committee, and this committee was in that great tradition. It called for a brick building four times the length of Westminster Abbey, with a dome 45 feet greater in diameter than that of St. Paul's. Fifteen million bricks would be required, but where they would be obtained in the time available and how they would be paid for were matters not on the agenda. The plan was adopted, but Cole left a loophole: An alternative plan could be used if one appeared.

It was now June 11, 1850, and the Great Exhibition, as it was called, was due to open May 1, 1851. Paxton and his friend, Mr. Ellis, Chairman of the Midland Railway, were observing tests of the new House of Commons for acoustics, which had proved unsatisfactory. Paxton feared another such mistake in the Great Exhibition, and he said that he had an idea. Mr. Ellis urged him to develop it, taking him to Lord Grenville and Mr. Cole, where Paxton undertook to have a plan ready in nine days. Exactly one week later Paxton was sitting as Chairman of the Works and Ways Committee of the Midland Railway while it was trying a pointsman for a minor offense, a large sheet of white blotting paper before him. The pointsman was let off with a fine of five shillings, but Paxton held up the blotting paper saying, "This is a design for the Great Industrial Exhibition to be held in Hyde Park." The sheet is now in the Victoria and Albert Museum, where one can easily see that the essentials of the construction are all indicated.

The plan was basically that of a greenhouse of unheard-of size: a width of 408 feet, a length of 1848 feet (against the 515 feet of St. Paul's Cathedral), and 108 feet to the highest point of the roof. It immediately captured the imagination, first of the committee and then of the public. An important, perhaps the crucial, point in its acceptance was that those wretched elms could be preserved by Paxton's plan, and by that one only.

There were objections — that the first strong wind would blow it down, that the glass would fall, that it would be intolerably hot, that moisture would constantly drip on the visitors, and so on and so on. These uninformed objections were countered in the seats of the mighty by Paxton's demonstrated ability to get done what he said he would do. The Queen may well have recalled the paths at Chatsworth on her visit 17 years before and the Duke of Wellington the tidying of its grounds on his visit of seven years previously.

In any event, the contract was signed on October 31, 1850, though fixing the columns had begun on September 26. The bare building was finished in 22 weeks and the fitting-out and painting in 15 more. The finished cost was £200,000, a fraction of the cost of a brick building of the same size.

The greatest innovation in Paxton's plan was that, for the first time, a prefabricated modular construction was used, with all girders, columns, gutters, and sash bars interchangeable. It was the first mass-produced building, just as the Model T Ford was the first mass-produced automobile. Another link with this great car was his design for special trolleys running on the frames; with them, 18,000 panes were placed in a week — a precursor of the assembly line. Many features of the Lily House found their way into the building, including columns which were also drain pipes. He reversed his plan for glass frames from that model, making moisture drain out of instead of into the structure.

Paxton was well aware of his indebtedness to *Victoria regia* by way of the Lily House. In a paper before the Fine Arts Society on November 13, 1850, he said, "Nature was the engineer. Nature has provided the leaf with longitudinal and transverse girders and supports that I, borrowing from it, have adopted in this building."

A major problem was the production in the time available of nearly one million square feet of glass in panes much larger than those commonly manufactured. The English tax on glass had restricted its use, and glass manufacturers there were far behind their counterparts on the Continent, since the tax had been repealed only in 1845. In any event, Belgian workers were brought over by the Chance Brothers, who produced the glass.

Apart from one minor strike, quickly settled, the only remaining problem concerned the juxtaposition of the glass and those troublesome elms. When the glass was nearly all in place, the elms were found to be full of sparrows. These were sure to soil the elegant attire of the visitors, and what if it should happen to the Queen! Desperate problems require desperate remedies. The first suggestion was shooting them, but the effect of the bullets on the glass was considered unfavorable. Next, bird-lime was proposed, to no one's satisfaction. In her extremity, the Queen summoned the Duke of Wellington to deal with the sparrows as he had with Napoleon at Waterloo. "Sparrow hawks, Ma'am," murmured the Iron Duke, whereupon the sparrows suddenly disappeared, no one knew why. But not quite all. When Hector Berlioz visited the Exhibition, he saw one lone sparrow and shared some crumbs from his biscuit with it — a gentle moment in the turbulent life of that composer.

Finally, all was ready for the grand opening ceremony on May 1st. As the strains of the "Hallelujah Chorus" burst forth, the Queen, closely attended by Prince Albert, led a procession of notables and declared the Exhibition open. The building did not fall down, nor did it drip or do any of the other dire things predicted.

At that point, the great structure leaves the Paxton story. When an architect completes a building, it passes beyond his jurisdiction and assumes a life of its own. Berenson comments, "So it is with each and every work of art. The moment it is created the creation is weaned from the creator."

The phenomenal success of the Great Exhibition from its opening was as much, or more, due to the building as to its contents. There were many reasons why the public became fascinated, but three are worth special comment. First, it was a status symbol of the British Empire as it approached its zenith. If the Duke of Devonshire required the Great Conservatory to symbolize his greatness, the British Empire needed an even grander symbol, and here it was. *Punch* caught this nuance exactly in a cartoon showing John Bull seated among the palms of the Exhibition, with the caption, "Mr. John Bull in his winter garden."

Second, it was quite simply — big. Eiffel, in relation to his tower, commented:

> There is an attraction and a charm in the colossal that is not subject to ordinary theories of art. Does anyone pretend that the Pyramids have so forcefully gripped the imagination of men through their artistic value? What are they after all but artificial hillocks? And yet what visitor can stand without reaction to their presence?

Third, and most important, it was fun. The social life of the emerging middle class was stodgy to a degree. In the evenings, Poppa read his newspaper, Mama was at the center table with her sewing, while one of the children read aloud from an "improving" book. Suddenly here was a glittering structure filled with exotic visitors and exhibits — as far from their solid, dark, gloomy buildings as fairyland. Again, it was *Punch* which caught the mood precisely.

Douglas Jerrold of its staff coined the name *Crystal Palace,* and this name has been used ever since, even in modern books on architectural history.

The fun aspect of the Great Exhibition had more to do with its phenomenal financial success than did the exhibits. The net profit was £186,437. With this a large tract of vacant land in London was bought to provide space for institutions of art and learning. This is why Exhibition Road is lined to this day with unlovely buildings housing learned institutions which continue to exert an international influence. Little was accomplished in fulfilling the stated objectives — the promotion of manufactures and world peace. Manufacturers in England and other countries went their way influenced by the Great Exhibition little or not at all. Certainly world peace was not attained. The Crimean War was less than three years off, and subsequent history is littered with wars and rumors of wars.

The people of London were in no mood to lose their Crystal Palace when the mandatory time of demolition was reached. It was rebuilt on Sydenham Hill, Paxton making some changes, especially a curvilinear roof like that of the Great Conservatory at Chatsworth. Exhibits were installed, concerts were given, and Paxton made a fine garden around it. The fortunes of the Crystal Palace fluctuated but gradually worsened. A fire destroyed the north transept on December 30, 1866, and the entire building went up in a Walpurgisnacht of flame on November 30, 1936. Even so, a survival of 85 years is not bad for a building intended to have a life of six months.

After the great effort of the Crystal Palace, Paxton's life ran on as calmly as his consuming energy would allow. His rewards were substantial: knighthood and an initial award of £5,000, raised to £20,000 as the result of public outcry. When this was added to his already substantial fortune, he became a wealthy man. He bought a country home, Rockhills, near Sydenham, where his friends came often, especially the Duke of Devonshire, who would drop in sometimes for a few days and sometimes for a few months.

Sarah came only occasionally, preferring to stay in the gardener's house at Chatsworth, putting into effect the plans for Chatsworth which continued to be the major concern of her husband. In fact, Sarah moved so little in society that she had been Lady Paxton for five years before she consented to be presented at court. But when she did, she did it in style: The presentation was made by that greatest of great ladies, Harriet, Duchess of Sutherland, Mistress of the Robes.

Of this singular but very happy marriage there were eight children, two boys and six girls. One son died in infancy and the other turned out badly, but the girls were all beautiful and intelligent, and made good marriages. As we have seen, there were people of ability among the grandchildren.

As befitted a man of prominence and wealth in those days, Paxton entered Parliament. There his career was undistinguished, the most memorable event being his effort to have civilians employed to build roads in the Crimea when the military failed. This proposal met with the predictable lack of success.

Meanwhile Paxton became what might be called architect-in-ordinary to the Rothschild family. He designed a huge house in Geneva for Baron Alphonse Rothschild; Ferrières, 25 miles from Paris, for Baron James; and Mentmore in Buckinghamshire for Baron Meyer. It must be recorded that modern taste favors his building in glass over that in more solid materials.

But a lifetime of frenetic activity at length exacted its toll, and Paxton's health began to fall. He died at Rockhills in his sixty-second year and was buried at Edensor, near Chatsworth, in the same churchyard as his great patron and friend, who had predeceased him — but at a respectful distance, for class distinctions persisted even to the grave.

In direct contradiction to Thurber's cynical remark with which I began, close study of Sir Joseph Paxton reveals him as a man of eminent sanity, of consuming energy channelled to useful purposes, of friendships made and kept. He was a man of utter dependability and integrity, whether he was dealing with the Queen or an undergardener. The only bad habit I discern was an uncontrollable urge to get up early in the morning. He would have made a desirable member of the Chicago Literary Club.

But what is left of Paxton's accomplishments? Of material objects very little. The Lily House was taken down long ago. *Victoria regia* is cultivated at Kew but at few other places. Changed economic conditions at the end of the First World War led to the dismantling of the Great Conservatory. Chatsworth and its gardens remain, though now in national possession. The Crystal Palace is no more. Mentmore has recently been refused by the Government in lieu of death duties, and its future is uncertain. The sale of its contents in 1977 was one of the most notable art auctions of this century, yielding over six million pounds, even after the most valuable paintings had been disposed of privately.

In 1935, Violet Markham's final comment was:

His versatility, so it seems to me, militated against his attaining the front rank in any one field. He took the popular imagination by storm with the dramatic incident of the Crystal Palace, the glass house that saved Prince Albert and the Great Exhibition of 1851 from ignominious collapse before the eyes of the world. His generation freely called him a genius, and so in a

manner he was. He made a large fortune; he was eminently successful. But he did not put his genius to permanent ends.

The four decades following that statement brought revolutions
in architecture as well as in socio-economic conditions. Paxton's influence has surfaced as a river long running underground emerges
again into the sunlight. In 1975 Christian Noberg-Schulz wrote:

> The form of the building represented a fundamentally new
> conception. . . . The size of the Crystal Palace may be defined as
> indeterminate, rendering obsolete Alberti's dictum that nothing
> might be added or taken away. . . . In this way the new technical
> possibilities set architecture free to frame new functions and
> forms of life.

This is the Age of Relevance. What possible relevance could the
works of this nineteenth-century Englishman have to Chicago in
1978? If you are on the north side of Chicago, go to Lincoln Park and
see his lengthened shadow on the planting between the Conservatory and the Zoo. If you are on the south side of Chicago, think how
much McCormick Place depends on the principles Paxton brought
together in the Crystal Palace. If you are in any part of Chicago, consider at what distance the glass high-rise buildings attempt to capture the glory of light which was the Crystal Palace. Not relevant,
you say? With respect I disagree.

BIBLIOGRAPHY

Allen, Mea. *Plants That Changed Our Gardens.* London: David and Charles, 1974.

Berenson, Bernard. *Aesthetics and History.* Garden City, N.Y.: Doubleday and Co., 1954.

Bernstein, Burton. *Thurber: A Biography.* New York: Ballentine Books Edition, 1976.

Bird, Anthony. *Paxton's Palace.* London: Cassell, 1976.

Gorer, Richard. *The Flower Garden in England.* London: B. T. Batsford, Ltd., 1975.

Hadfield, Miles. *Gardening in Britain.* Hutchinson of London, 1960.

Harriss, Joseph. *The Tallest Tower: Eiffel and the Belle Epoque.* Boston: Houghton Mifflin Co., 1975.

Healey, B. J. *The Plant Hunters.* New York: Charles Scribner's Sons, 1975.

Hibbert, Christopher. *London: The Biography of a City.* New York: William Morrow and Co., Inc., 1969.

Lemmon, Kenneth. *The Covered Garden.* London: Museum Press, 1962.

Lemmon, Kenneth. *The Golden Age of Plant Hunters.* London: J.M. Dent and Sons, Ltd., 1968.

Longford, Elizabeth. *Queen Victoria: Born to Succeed.* New York: Harper and Row, 1964.

Longford, Elizabeth. *Wellington: Pillar of State.* New York: Harper and Row, 1972.

Markham, Violet R. *Paxton and the Bachelor Duke.* London: Hodder and Stoughton, Ltd., 1935.

Norberg-Schulz, Christian. *Meaning in Western Architecture.* New York: Praeger Publishers, 1975.

Priestley, J. B. *Victoria's Heyday.* London: William Heinemann, 1972. (cited from Penguin ed., 1974.)

Sandburg, Carl. *Abraham Lincoln: The Prairie Years and the War Years.* New York: Harcourt Brace Jovanovich, Harvest Edition, 1974.

Woodham-Smith, Cecil. *Queen Victoria: From Her Birth to the Death of the Prince Consort.* New York: Alfred A. Knopf, 1972.

CHAPTER THREE

How Fair the Meadows Are Today

IN THE THIRD ACT of *Parsifal*, the hero exclaims:

> *How fair the fields and meadows are to-day!. . . .*
> *These tendrils bursting with blossom,*
> *Whose scent recalls my childhood's days*
> *And speaks of loving trust to me.*

and Gurnemanz responds:

> *That is Good Friday's spell, my lord!*

The resurgence of nature from its winter sleep has from time immemorial stirred the deepest emotions of the human race. By tradition, it turns the thoughts of the young man to his beloved and stimulates artists to great achievements. To capture the floodtide of spring, Schubert composed *Das Lied im Grünen;* Botticelli painted the *Primavera;* Wordsworth wrote *I Wandered Lonely as a Cloud.*

Read at the Chicago Literary Club on Ladies' Night, May 21, 1973.

Spring is not traditionally the stimulus for great deeds of science and exploration, but there are exceptions. One spring day in the early eighteenth century, a Philadelphia Quaker farmer was ploughing a field. As he later wrote, he suddenly saw a daisy and thought, "It is a shame that thee should destroy so many plants without being acquainted with their structure and uses." This idea seized him with such force that he set upon a course of action from which he did not deviate for the rest of his long life. It was to lead him to create a revolution in the gardens of England and Europe, to receive the admiration and friendship of the greatest botanists in the world, to be appointed King's Botanist by George III of England. He was to raise and train a son whose book would exert a significant influence on the entire Romantic Movement in English poetry. A good day's ploughing!

John Bartram, for such was his name, was the first native-born American botanist to acquire an international reputation and was the founder of the first botanic garden in North America. Born in Darby, Pennsylvania in 1699, he was of Quaker ancestry. His grandfather immigrated from Derbyshire, England, in 1682, the year in which the city of Philadelphia was founded. One of the group led by William Penn, John grew up among devout Quakers, including Benjamin Franklin, whose friendship was later to be crucial in his development as a botanist.

Bartram's formal education was only that minimum which the country school could provide, but he taught himself Latin and Greek by buying the few grammars and classics in those languages which his slim pocket-book would allow. Early he was inclined toward medicine, and such knowledge of it as he could acquire probably increased his interest in plants, for herbs were then almost the only available drugs. Meanwhile, his success as a farmer was becoming notable, for he raised 38 bushels of wheat on the same amount of land as his neighbors could grow 20. Above middle height and very strong, his excellent husbandry and gentle piety quickly established him in the Quaker community.

In 1729 he married and the next year he completed a house on the banks of the Schuylkill River, building it with his own hands. By this time his boyhood interest in plants had become transformed into a passion. The change may not have been as sudden as the daisy incident suggests, but a rapid change there certainly was. Franklin, in his incisive and kindly way, recognized that John's enthusiasm was coupled with extraordinary powers of observation. It was Franklin's international contacts which enabled him to put John's talents to work, for the Quakers in England included several able botanists. In the early 1730s, Franklin called John to the attention of Peter Collinson, a draper in London who was developing what we would now call a nursery business, sending rarities to the great houses of the nobility. By 1735 Collinson had contracted with John to collect seeds — "100 species in a box at five guineas each." Thus began John's trips into country which was unexplored botanically and sometimes totally unknown. The journeys were to continue until old age, and the later explorations were more arduous than the early ones. For the first eight years, he traveled in Pennsylvania, Delaware, and Virginia, but 1743 saw him making a trip to the shore of Lake Ontario and what is now Oswego.

These journeys were physically taxing and full of danger. It was his custom to set out on horseback before first light and ride until sunset, his keen eye identifying new species and his collecting hand filling his baskets with unknown plants. There were at best only rough paths, and much of the time he was in complete wilderness. On longer journeys, such as those to what is now New York State, there was always the hazard of Indian attack, for the tribes had at best undependable relations with white people.

When he returned from a journey, he planted his discoveries in his garden to grow them before shipment, whether plants or seeds. In exchange, Collinson would send him European plants not known on this side of the Atlantic. These he also incorporated in his plantings until they became a botanic garden, not only the first in North America but also probably the first anywhere intended to include both native and exotic species. John Bartram thus set a pattern which most American botanic gardens follow to this day. The Morton Arboretum is an excellent example. The Bartram Garden is the direct ancestor of our emerging Chicago Botanic Garden.

Collinson rapidly found this American botanist a source of great wealth. He sold garden boxes at 5 guineas each to the Dukes of Bedford, Marlborough, Norfolk, and Richmond; the Earls of Bute, Leicester, and Lincoln; well-known private gardeners such as William Penn and Phillip Miller of the Chelsea Physic Garden; and Lord Petrie, Collinson's first and most loyal customer.

But not much money came the other way. On rare occasions, Collinson sent £10 or £20 in half-pence, but he usually contented himself with occasional presents of clothing for John, dresses for his wife, and toys for his children. Their relations were always amicable despite Collinson's periodic goading to send more, and yet more. Bertram did not grudge him his wealth, and Collinson sought honors and contacts with learned men for Bartram. Financially, Bartram suffered because his farm had to be neglected in his long absences. Local recognition was beginning, for in 1744 he was chosen as one of the nine original members of the American Philosophical Society. His home became the first port of call for European botanists doing their own exploring. One was Peter Kalm, the

Swedish botanist, then beginning his own wide-reaching travels in North America. Bartram's advice helped him on his way to the discoveries which made him one of the great botanic explorers. In 1750 John sent a manuscript describing his observations to Collinson, who had it published the next year without his knowledge.

In one way, Bartram failed Collinson, who wanted zoological specimens and all sorts of curiosities as well as plants. Bartram sent fossils, turtle eggs, butterflies, and humming birds' nests but no skins of animals or birds. That gentle Quaker could not bring himself to kill.

In 1753 John Bartram traveled up the Delaware River to the Catskills, then almost unexplored forest with undergrowth containing interesting and unknown plants of garden value, a region which he later visited a second time. I grew up in this region and know at first hand the botanical riches which awaited him. This was the first journey on which he took his son William, now aged fifteen. Of John's eleven children, it was William who gave promise of botanical accomplishment. He had the power of observation of his father, who gave him the best education Philadelphia afforded and taught him the botanical skills he had acquired in his years of study and travel. From then on, William was his father's constant companion in exploration and was trained to continue on his own.

In 1755 they traveled together to Connecticut. At about this time John began correspondence with Dr. Alexander Garden of Charleston, South Carolina, an authority on southern plants and a contributor to knowledge of them. In 1760 John visited Dr. Garden for 18 days. Thereafter most of the Bartram explorations were to the south of Philadelphia — across the Blue Ridge Mountains, to Carolina, Georgia, Florida, and elsewhere. John's journal, *A Description of East Florida,* was published in London in 1769.

Meanwhile, international honors were piling up. The most important was John's appointment as King's Botanist in 1765, for it carried a yearly stipend of £50. Collinson secured the appointment for him with the help and encouragement of Franklin. This was the greatest financial reward Collinson gave him (although it did not come from Collinson's pocket). John had to send the King plants, minerals, and other curiosities at frequent intervals. Considering the London prices for such objects, His Majesty probably got a good bargain. John was also elected to the Royal Academy of Sciences of Stockholm in 1769, and in 1772 the Society of Gentlemen in Edinburgh gave him a gold medal. Significant as these honors were, there is no evidence that they made a deep impression on him, for worldly pride was a deadly sin to this devout Quaker. He expressed his motivation in a letter to Collinson: "My head runs all upon the works of God, in Nature. It is through that telescope I see God in His glory."

In 1768 Collinson died at the age of 74, and the garden of Dr. John Fothergill at Upton, Essex, became the center for American introductions. Dr. Fothergill had already corresponded with the Bartrams and was to become William's patron. Like the other Bartram friends and patrons, Dr. Fothergill was a Quaker, another of those who sought to know God as He was manifest in nature.

John's passion for botanical discovery did not diminish, even though he was nearly 70. His efforts at this age began to alarm Franklin. On January 9, 1769, he wrote John from London:

> I hope your health continues — as does mine, hitherto; but I wish you would now decline your long and dangerous peregrinations, in search of your plants, and remain safe and quiet at home.

But a lifetime of vigorous health had left him convinced that illness and the infirmities of age were for other people. Franklin's suggestion was that the old man should write a natural history of North America. No one at that time was better fitted to do so, but the literary life was not for John. He worked at his garden and continued to send shipments of plants until his death at 78, just at the time when Washington's army was moving into winter quarters at Valley Forge.

The terms of John's will are important, since they clarify his estimate of his practical namesake and his talented but undedicated son William. These have often been misquoted and quite extraordinary conclusions drawn. Through the kindness of Mrs. Charles Rupp, I have been able to examine the original manuscript of the will and the certificate of probate, both now in the Philadelphia Historical Society. It is dated January 17, 1772. William received a legacy of £200, his fair share of the estate, without any obligations. Son Isaac had the same amount but was to contribute £10 per year to his mother. The crucial bequest was to his namesake John:

> I give and bequeath to my son John Bartram all my plantation whereon we live, situated between David Gibson's Land and My Son James Bartram's Land with all the Appurtenances belonging to it, both Upland and Meadows, to him and to his heirs forever, he paying his mother yearly the sum of £10 and is to find her sufficient firewood cut and handed to the door of her kitchen and keep her a cow and horse Winter and Summer on good Grass or Hay.

The affectionate concern for his wife's welfare speaks volumes for the sort of man John Bartram was. The will also makes clear that the father had too little trust in William's practicality to pass on to him responsibility for either his garden or his widow.

William, as we have seen, was well educated not only in schools but in practical botany by his travels with his father. He had inherited the parental sharpness of observation and was fitted in many ways to carry on the family tradition in botanical exploration. But his greatest gifts were ones that John did not possess: the ability to draw plants and animals well and literary talents which amounted to genius. He made a trip to London, which his father had not been able to do. There the nobility extravagantly praised his drawings. However, it was Dr. Fothergill who decided that William's talents should be gainfully employed. Besides finding patrons for his drawings, he sponsored an expedition to the southeast, including the Carolinas and Florida. These travels became prolonged and William did not return until January, 1777, only a few months before his father's death. His plants and drawings could no longer go to England because the American Revolution was in progress. When it was over, his father and Dr. Fothergill were dead, and there was nobody to inspire or goad him into exploration. This was a pity, for William was an excellent observer, so much so that some of his reports which were doubted for many years have later been confirmed, sometimes after as much as a century and a half. He led a peaceful existence in the old home, admired and visited by a wide circle of friends. This esteem led to his election to the American Philosophical Society in 1786. However, he had declined the offer of a professorship of botany at the University of the State of Pennsylvania four years earlier on the grounds of ill health. He occupied much time in turning the journals of his trip to the southeast into a book, published in 1791. Two years later, Thomas Jefferson took a house nearby for the summer and an enduring friendship developed between the two.

Jefferson's knowledge and skill in horticulture are often forgotten, but they make him a major figure in American garden history. One of the important reasons for Jefferson's strong sponsorship of the Lewis and Clark Expedition was his desire to see what plants might be brought back for gardens. William turned down Jefferson's urgent personal request to be the botanist of that expedition on the grounds of ill health and advanced age. He was 65, an age at which his father was actively exploring. But William preferred to sit at home and join John, Jr., in preparing a catalog of the garden, corresponding with friends, advising and helping others to explore what he no longer cared to investigate himself. Despite his complaints about his health, he lived on until 1823, dying, a lifelong bachelor, at 84.

The impact of the Bartrams on horticulture is hard to over-estimate. It depended on several factors which interacted with one another. In the eighteenth century, English gardens underwent a complete revolution. In the early years of the century, their design was uncompromisingly formal, with geometric beds and clipped shrubs as their basic elements. By the time of John Bartram's death in 1777, all this had been swept away by such garden designers as Capability Brown, and the ideal had become "nature improved." This left large expanses to be filled with plants. Since novelty was in the air, new and unusual plants were required in unprecedented numbers.

The Bartrams' introductions came along just in time to fill this need and had the attraction of originating in a strange and remote country. There is probably no part of the world today as unexplored as North America between its east and west coasts was in the Bartrams' time. Interest in this vast colony in uneasy association with the Mother Country was intense and was abetted by the numerous wealthy English collectors who amassed any sort of odd specimen for their "cabinets" — mineral, zoological, or anthropological.

Bartram, through Collinson and Fothergill, offered them equally strange plants to make their gardens as curious as their collections of dried specimens. Most of them came from climates sufficiently like Britain to ensure their survival in the open. The result was that a cult for things American grew up which has not entirely disappeared from English horticulture. I noted at the April 18, 1972, show of the Royal Horticultural Society: "Class 23. 3 pans rock plants, distinct, from the continent of America (excluding garden hybrids)."

These considerations would apply equally to any of the European explorers of North America at that time. There were several reasons why the Bartram contribution was different. In the first place, most of the other botanists were visitors for at most two or three years, while John collected over more than 40 years and William extended the period by another generation. This, together with John's consuming energy and dedication, resulted in the introduction of an almost incredible number of new species to Georgian England. They were recorded at Kew, usually without attribution, sometimes as "Bartram" but rarely with any specification as to which Bartram. This makes any exact calculation impossible and suggests that the largest estimates are the most reliable. A reasonable estimate is that of 300 new plants introduced into England between 1735 and 1780, the Bartrams were responsible for at least two-thirds. Nearly all of these were sent by John. William seldom bestirred himself to ship new plants, but he certainly introduced the oak-leafed hydrangea, which is a valued shrub in contemporary gardens throughout the world. Impressive as these numbers are, they explain only a small part of the result. It was not for nothing that Linneas praised John's powers of observation, calling him "the greatest Natural Botanist in the world." Among the plants introduced were the American rhododendrons, lilies, irises, beebalm, and many others which are still garden favorites. Yet even Bartram could not always tell what would be desirable on the other side of the Atlantic. On December 18, 1742, he wrote to Collinson:

> The Doctor's famous *Lychnis,* which thee has dignified so highly, is, I think unworthy of that character. Our swamps and low grounds are full of them. I had so contemptible an opinion of it, as to not think it worth sending, nor afford it room in my garden; but I suppose, by thy account, your climate agreeth so well, that it is much improved.

The Bartram introduction which has received most comment is a small tree, or large shrub, which is usually called *Franklinia,* in honor of Benjamin Franklin, but has the botanical name *Gordonia altamaha.* It had almost no influence on English gardens, for it is hardy only in the mildest British climates, but it grows well enough in the warmer parts of the European continent and flourishes in American gardens from Philadelphia south. White flowers begin to appear in August and in favorable years continue after the leaves have taken on the reds of autumn. Specimens are currently available from American nurseries; it should be more widely planted in gardens where it is hardy.

But the reason for the special interest in this plant is the puzzle it poses in ecology. On October 1, 1765, John was traveling along the Altamaha River in Georgia with William, then fifteen. Near Fort Barrington they came upon a grove of these trees, but found no more. Eight years later, William located the grove again and took cuttings. It was seen in the wild by Marshall in 1790 and by Lyon in 1803. These four sightings of isolated specimens are the only occasions on which *Franklinia* has been found in the wild state, and all the plants in the gardens of the world derive from William's cuttings in 1773. There have been other reports of discovery in the wild, but all have proved false and some ludicrous. In 1929, for example, a government forester made such a report, and it took careful study to discover that the sighting actually was in a dream.

Consider what this implies. The woods of Georgia were not changing rapidly in the eighteenth and early nineteenth centuries, so man's ravages are not the explanation. Neither the Bartrams nor other explorers found it elsewhere. In the wild, the distribution was confined to a small area, but it grows freely over large regions under garden conditions. For the same reason, it is not a species which has lost its capacity for growth, a condition which causes the extinction of some varieties of plants and animals. Solution of this enigma might give a clue to larger ecological problems. What we have, however, is speculation and a voluminous literature.

Important as the Bartrams' first introductions were, they explain only a small part of their contribution to the revolution in English gardens. From the standpoint of practical horticulture, a plant known only from dried specimens in herbaria is without value. One represented by a few examples in the garden of a jealous collector makes little more impact on horticulture in general. What the Bartrams, and especially John, did was to send not only their own introductions but those of others in such volume that the plants could be widely used and firmly established as garden subjects. Other explorers might spend two or three years in a collecting area and have one or at most a few chances to send material. Plants had to go by whatever ship was available, at any season of the year and attended by a crew that was usually indifferent, if not hostile. Losses averaged ninety per cent in the eighteenth century. The Bartrams lived permanently near collecting areas and established the plants in John's garden. Seeds or live plants could be sent again and again until success was achieved.

There were several reasons for the heavy losses and for John Bartram's success in overcoming them more often than others. One was that the methods of preparing seeds and plants for shipment were at best inadequate and at worst ridiculous to modern eyes. The procedure recommended to John by Collinson was more sensible than most. In a letter of January 20, 1735, Collinson wrote:

> A great many may be put in a box 20 inches or 2 feet square, and 15 or 16 inches high: . . . and a foot in earth is enough. This may be put under the Captain's bed, or set in the cabin, if it is sent in October or November. Nail a few narrow laths across it, to keep the cats from scratching it.

This letter also indicates other factors that John could control but other explorers could not. Since the seeds and plants would usually have been grown for some time in the Bartram garden, they could be dispatched on their two- or three-month voyage at the most favorable time. When sent in late fall, they would arrive in England early in the new year and could be brought on in greenhouses for spring planting in the open.

John also knew the sea captains and could select those who understood plants and were interested in them. The names of some forty of these sea captains are recorded; they deserve a footnote in history. But even so, there were great losses. If the cats ruined a shipment, John sent a second. If the rats escaped the cats and destroyed the plants, he sent a third. If the sailors sabotaged the fourth, he sent another until the novel plants were established in quantity. Collinson also kept him informed of the plants which were most in demand. Such plants as Solomon's seal, lady slippers, American lilies, goldenrod, and white locusts were shipped on many occasions. There were repeat shipments of many plants which grew well in England but did not ripen seeds in the cool summers there. On March 3, 1741, Collinson wrote:

> ... for, though mine grows strong, and flowers finely, yet our summers are not sufficient to bring its seed to perfection. ... For this reason, thee must send all sorts of herbaceous seeds over again, as they happen ripe in they way.

As we have seen, the prices of such plants were enormous, and Collinson received as much financial reward as fame, though the Bartrams did not. Such valuable possessions in the open garden were a temptation to robbery. Sale of rare American plants of undisclosed provenance had its problems, but there were collectors more avid than scrupulous. Two men could carry away enough in a night to buy each a comfortable house and keep them in comfort for years. If the robbers were caught, penalties were severe — deportation usual and hanging possible. These robberies are in a different class from present-day vandalism in gardens and parks. They are more closely comparable to modern art robberies, since they involved abduction of easily moved objects of great value and sale to enthusiasts who asked no questions.

Robbers at length found Collinson's garden. On August 21, 1766, he wrote John:

> I am ruined with two great robberies, so I cannot stand in any competition. Once, I bore the bell; but now, I very humbly condescend to be on an equal footing with my neighbors.

After Collinson's death, his son inherited the estate. More robberies in rapid succession led him to abandon the house and garden and take up residence elsewhere. The house was eventually demolished and the site is now occupied by the Mill Hill School. On the grounds, however, there are still a few trees planted by Collinson: some cedars, a tulip tree, a plane, and a deciduous cypress. These are piously tended by the school but are small reminders of a great garden.

Dr. Fothergill's estate, West Ham Park in Essex, is more or less intact and remains a valuable source for the study of American plants. The Bartrams' house and garden also still exist. The younger John, to whom John the elder had willed them, died in 1812. Thereafter they were tended by granddaughter Ann (or Nancy, as she was usually called) and her husband, Colonel Carr. Ann was a good botanist in her own right and maintained the standard of the garden as long as she lived. But eventually the Carrs too, were no more, and weeds, tall grass, and dead branches took over the garden. Fortunately the City of Philadelphia bought the house and garden in 1891 for a memorial and for use as a park. It is now administered and maintained jointly by the Fairmount Park authorities and the John Bartram Association. It has been declared a National Historic Monument by the United States Government.

The house which John Bartram built with his own hands in 1730 is in fine condition, more because of John's workmanship than through restoration. The visitor senses the solid construction and admires the comfortable rooms safe from winter cold and summer heat and the stones that John carved with images of plants and set in the wall. The garden, now smaller than in the Bartrams' time, is ringed about with trees of species they collected, and some of the undergrowth is *Franklinia*. One yellow-wood is probably the only specimen still alive which was growing there in John Bartram's time, but several very large trees may have been planted by William. The protective belt has closed the vista to the Schuylkill, but this is just as well, since the river is now polluted and on the opposite bank modern industrialism intrudes. Of all the historic sites in and around Philadelphia, this island of peace evokes the life of the eighteenth century and the unpretentious but distinguished men who lived there more immediately than any other of the historical sites of that city.

One sort of memorial which explorers cherish more than almost any other is the naming of a plant or animal for them. The Bartrams' friends and patrons fared very well in this regard — but not the Bartrams. Peter Kalm is known to every knowledgeable gardener, for *Kalmia latifolia* is the mountain laurel, a beloved shrub in the wild over a wide area of the United States and a cherished ornamental in the gardens of the world. *Fothergilla* is a genus of American witch hazels, some members of which are prized in the English spring gardens of today. *Gardenia* for Dr. Garden, the Bartrams' Charleston friend, hardly needs explanation. *Collinsonia canadensis* was the name given by Linneas to our common stoneroot, which we think of as a weed but which was a popular garden subject in England in Collinson's time. Collinson placed more value on such worldly honors than was entirely appropriate for a Quaker, but in this matter he wrote John on September 2, 1739, "But I think it should rather be *Bartramia*; for I had it in the very first seeds thee sent me."

Linneas intended to name a plant *Bartramia,* but it proved already to be otherwise named. After John's death, this term was applied to a lowly moss, of no horticultural value. Not a very good tribute to the man who made so many of the others possible.

William's drawings also are preserved. The most important collection consists of those made for Dr. Fothergill. These were bound in an album which was purchased by Sir Joseph Banks after Fothergill's death in 1780. In 1827 the album came to the Natural History Division of the British Museum. It was reproduced in a handsome edition in 1968. Other drawings are scattered in English and American collections.

These plant drawings, extravagantly praised at the time, are very accurate in botanical detail but seem less successful in decorative value or in catching the essence of the plants than those of Catesby and other artists of the time. For instance, William's plate of the *Franklinia* gives the blossom the solidity of a camellia, but the effect of this tree in bloom is like a flock of white butterflies passing through dense foliage. The drawings of animals are able for their time and for historical record, but most of them now appear merely quaint.

Such survivals are completely overshadowed by the journals of John and William, with their influence on science and poetry. John's surviving journals of his journeys had been published by Collinson but others were lost in the inevitable accidents of hazardous travel. Those published are one of the richest and most accurate sources of information about eighteenth-century American climate and ecology available, but as literature they have the lack of stylistic distinction expected in a modern scientific publication. For instance, the entry for the day on which *Franklinia* was first found reads:

> *October 1, 1765* Fine, clear, cool morning. Thermometer 56, P.M. 68. This day's riding was very bad through bay swamps. . . . This day's journey of twenty miles was all low, flat ground, the highest piney ground seldom above three or four foot perpendi-

cular above the swamps. . . . This day we found several very curious shrubs, one bearing beautiful good fruit.

No mention, you note, of the great discovery.

The writings of William are quite another matter. In his many
years of retirement, he used the journals which he had kept on his
journeys through the Carolinas, Georgia, and Florida as the basis for
a book of travel. The process of revision and polishing went on for
nearly 20 years, but unlike many men of William's temperament, he
finally brought the book to publication in 1791. It was quickly recognized that here was a notable literary achievement. The vividness of
the imagery is extraordinary, and reading it today gives one a sense
of immediacy that makes one feel almost an eyewitness. It is generally regarded as perhaps the finest book on North American travel
produced in the eighteenth century.

When an edition was brought out in England two years later, it
seized the imagination of the group of lyric poets who were then
producing their finest work. Reasons for English interest in America
have already received comment. William brought a feeling for this
strange region to writers who were shaping the Romantic Movement
and receptive to the odd and remote. Coleridge was the first to fall
under the spell. In introducing the *Travels* to Wordsworth, Coleridge
called it "not a Book of Travels properly speaking, but a series of poems, Chiefly descriptive, occasioned by the objects which the Trav-
eler observed."

William's images at once found their way into English poetry.
Wordsworth's long ballad *Ruth* is based almost wholly on the *Travels*,
and passages from *The Prelude* have the same source, as does *She
Was a Phantom of Delight*. Even Wordsworth's famous daffodils owe
much to William's "vegetable beauties" which "by the mountain

breezes are tossed about." Southey, the Poet Laureate, used the book for images of subtropical birds and plants. His poem *Madoc* describes a wild turkey in a magnolia tree, an incident stemming directly from the *Travels*.

But it was Coleridge who was the most deeply stirred. Several of his less familiar poems are directly related to William's book but, more importantly, it was a major source for *The Rime of the Ancient Mariner* and *Kubla Khan*. Here we have a guide, for John Livingston Lowes's *The Road to Xanadu* ostensibly explored the sources of these two poems. In doing so, Lowes produced one of the finest studies of the process of literary creation that has ever been written. The reader can see how William's images have fallen into Coleridge's unconscious and been recalled by associations in new forms and combinations. This process comes out clearly in *The Rime of the Ancient Mariner*. Here is an example dealing with subtropical thunderstorms:

> The rain came down with such rapidity and fell in such quantities, that every object was totally obscured, excepting the continuous streams or rivers of lightning pouring from the clouds. . . . The hurricane comes on roaring. . . . the dark cloud opens over my head, diveloping [sic] a vast river of the etherial fire. . . . when instantly the lightning, as it were, opening a fiery chasm in the black cloud, darted with inconceivable rapidity on the trunk of a large pine tree.

And Coleridge transmutes these same images into lyric poetry:

> *The thick black cloud was cleft, and still*
> *The Moon was at its side:*

65

Like waters shot from some high crag,
The lightning fell with never a jag,
A river steep and wide.

William was Coleridge's authority also on tropical fishes, alligators, American Indians, and other exotic subjects, but he also gave Coleridge a new way of seeing familiar objects. Of the moon and the process of transformation Lowes comments:

> "At length, a silver thread alone encircles her temples," Bartram had written of his moon. And so when Coleridge saw at Keswick, on that eventful night for the three friends, the dark of the moon rimmed with its circum-ambient brightness, it too was "circled by a silver thread." Leaving aside the architectonics and the magic, it is hard to set a limit to the potency of that deep, thronging reservoir of latent memories, prompt at a touch to flow in upon the impulses of immediate impression.

The imagery of *Kubla Khan* is to a surprising extent direct from the *Travels*. William had written of "Chrystal fountains," of meandering rivers, of caverns, of an "inchanting little Isle of Palms." Here again the vivid images of the American explorer crossed the Atlantic to be moulded by Coleridge's genius into the pure gold of lyric poetry. As Lowes says:

> For the imagination never operates in a vacuum. Its stuff is always fact of some order, somehow experienced; its product is that fact transmitted. . . . When . . . the stuff that Professors and Doctors are made of has been distilled into quintessential poetry, then the passing miracle of Creation has been performed.

Beyond supplying raw materials for this transmutation, the Bartrams provided an impetus in the garden as well as in the library for the intense observation and palpable closeness to nature which is at the heart of the Romantic tradition in English poetry. An Englishman, Brian Dunning, has commented:

> The philosophy of nature translated into a way of life by the Bartrams, father and son, went to the heart of English literature. The belief that a humble daisy is beautiful and significant in its own right lies at the root of much of our thinking, even at the present time. It is strange indeed that two Americans should have been responsible for part of the "Englishness" of the English.

Yet in many ways, John Bartram was characteristically American. There is a type of individual which has on rare occasions appeared in many countries but sufficiently more often in the United States as to seem a national characteristic. These are men with little or no formal education who have become obsessed by an idea and followed wherever it led. If a niche in history comes to them, it is unsought. Some have amassed large fortunes without regard to means, like Jay Gould; some have participated in great events of history and have received international respect and admiration, like Abraham Lincoln; others are known only to a small group of specialists, like Daniel B. Updike, the distinguished authority on printing types. John Bartram as an individual is familiar largely to botanists and horticulturists, but the plants he brought into cultivation give him kinship with all who make a garden.

William Bartram was one of a sort of man found in all civilizations. His learning and talents were great but unfocussed. When

67

such a man — and there have been a few — finally produces a work of summation, it has a richness and influence which hurried and self-seeking efforts do not.

It is well in this our springtime to think of the Bartrams, father and son. Their memory will give a deepened perception as we plant our gardens or walk through the countryside and sense again how fair the meadows are today.

CHAPTER FOUR

A Voyage of 1052 Days

⌒

ENGLISH SOCIAL HISTORY in the reign of George III is a study in contrasts. The rich were very rich and the poor were very poor, with little middle ground and less mobility from one class to the other. For the nobility and landed gentry there was only one respectable source of wealth: the ownership of land, despite the fact that many of the great gentlemen were absentee landlords who seldom or never visited the estates which provided their incomes. The appearance and dress of the upper classes are familiar through the paintings of Reynolds and Gainsborough, while those of both classes were recorded less gently in the paintings of Hogarth and the caricatures of Gillray and Cruickshank. One might suppose that wealth so largely based on land ownership would be stable, but that was not always the case. There is the contrast between the estates which expanded and those which were depleted beyond retrieval, mostly through two mechanisms: gambling and high living in London or the extravagant building of the great country houses which are still a chief glory of England. But this same class also produced the

---

Read at the Chicago Literary Club on May 17, 1982.

Georgian statesmen and politicians — some wise, like Edmund Burke, some not so wise, like Lord North — whose advice to the King made an important contribution to the situation in which we find ourselves tonight, as citizens of the United States of America and not subjects of Queen Elizabeth II. A few combined both forms of activity, such as Charles James Fox, equally remembered as statesman and man-about-town. Contributions to science were not expected from the Georgian upper classes, but there were exceptions. One such was Joseph Banks.

On a chilly, rainy February night in 1744, a strong boy was born to William and Sarah Banks in their London house on Argyll Street in Westminister, far from the family estate, Revesby Abbey, in Lincolnshire. The baby was named Joseph for his great-grandfather, who had done much to enlarge the vast fortune to which the newborn son was now heir.

The Bankses belonged to the landed gentry, not the nobility, though there were noble connections through marriage into the Greville family and those of the Earls of Stanhope and Exeter. It was expected that Joseph would continue the family tradition, which combined management of the Lincolnshire estate with public service and sitting in Parliament.

Joseph spent his early childhood at Revesby Abbey, where his interests were in the fields around him and his favorite diversion was fishing. These activities accorded better with those of his strong-minded mother than those of his father, who insisted upon a classical education. At the age of nine, he entered Harrow, where his scholastic record was so appalling that four years later he was transferred to Eton, where it was not much better. But it was at Eton at the age of fifteen that his true interests in botany came into focus.

At 17, Banks entered Christ Church, Oxford. His record in the classical curriculum there was no better than at Harrow and Eton, but his interest in botanical science was intense. The professor of botany gave no lectures, but suggested that he apply to Israel Lyons at Cambridge. Lyons came to Oxford, where he was supported by Banks's own funds, the first use of the Banks fortune for natural science.

Banks's father died when Joseph was 18. The estate was astutely managed by his mother until he reached his majority three years later, in 1764. Then in possession of a great fortune, he decided from the first that it should be devoted to the advancement of science, particularly botany; he considered that he held it in trust and not for himself alone. The amount of his yearly income is not precisely known, but an informed estimate would be £10,000 per year. At the standard rate, this would be the equivalent of $50,000. Inflation between 1764 and 1982 is at least 30 times and probably more. The purchasing power of his income in 1982 would be at least $1,500,000 per year — without income tax, of course.

Joseph left Oxford without taking a degree and settled in London. It was at this point that a young man of his position was expected to make the Grand Tour of the Continent, seeing historic monuments, learning the social graces of foreign society, and collecting works of art to enrich the great houses in London and the countryside. Banks, however, had other ideas. His interests lay in botany and scientific collecting; he decided to do his traveling in pursuit of these objectives.

Only two years later he seized the opportunity to make a seven months' voyage to Newfoundland and Labrador, then largely unexplored. Despite problems with seasickness, Banks pursued his collecting activities with energy and brought back botanical specimens which were the start of his herbarium, later to become so large; there were also examples of animals, birds, and fishes, many new to

European science. But he also proved his adaptability to harsh conditions and his capacity to get along with sailors and with the native populations, receiving their good will and relishing their food. His journal records his reaction to fish chowder: "The chief food of the poorer and, when well made, a luxury that the rich, even in England, at least in my opinion, might be fond of." Since it is one of my favorite foods, I applaud his judgment. The importance of his discoveries brought immediate recognition, and even before his return he was elected a Fellow of the Royal Society, when he was only twenty-three. Indeed, Banks had a double qualification for that honor: He was an academically trained botanist and a proven field collector. At the same time, he was a very wealthy man. The Royal Society was then in a precarious financial position, which led to the election of some rich amateurs who might help the treasury when needed.

Two years later, in 1768, the governments of several European countries conjointly planned a series of expeditions to observe the transit of Venus which would occur the next year, 1769. The English government undertook to observe it in the South Seas in the course of a voyage sponsored jointly by the Admiralty and the Royal Society. The transit of Venus is the passage of that body over the disk of the sun, which can be seen only when the earth and Venus pass a node of the orbit at nearly the same time. From the time of the transit the distance of the sun from the earth can be calculated, a figure thought to be an important aid to navigation. Since the transit occurs only four times in 243 years and the next was not due until 1874, 105 years later, correct observations were important to astronomers and vital to governments.

Having tasted exploration and collecting in distant lands, Banks was eager for more. He sought permission to go on the journey and obtained it, even though such voyages usually did not include a naturalist. However, a few precedents existed, and there were several reasons why Banks's request succeeded. He was already well known as an able and generous Fellow of the Royal Society, if a somewhat domineering one. Also there was the question of finances. The Royal Society had petitioned the King for a ship and £4,000, which was barely enough. Banks was willing to pay his own way and to help the expedition, his contribution amounting to £10,000, a great sum but equal only to his income for one year.

It was also clear that Banks's experience in Newfoundland and Labrador gave him unusual qualifications in planning the natural history undertakings on a long journey. These he exploited to the full, taking along a fine library and the most effective forms of equipment for preserving specimens of flora and fauna.

The Admiralty turned down the choice of the Royal Society for the leader of the expedition and selected James Cook, who was known only in naval circles but who had distinguished himself by carrying General Wolfe for his successful storming of Quebec and by his work as a marine surveyor. He asked for and obtained a collier because of its shallow draft, valuable in uncharted seas of variable and unknown depth. The collier was renamed the *Endeavour,* and as such has sailed into history.

Banks traveled in style. His party included three artists and an assistant draftsman, as well as two servants from Revesby and — true Englishman that he was — his two faithful greyhounds. But his chief assistant was Daniel Solander, an outstanding naturalist then working at the British Museum and a favorite pupil of Linnaeus.

Among the most important arrangements for the journey were the measures to prevent scurvy, the great scourge of long sea voyages at that time. Cook depended on sauerkraut and Banks on lemon juice taken with brandy. Both were effective, and the expedition wholly escaped that hazard.

At last all was ready, and on August 25, 1768, the *Endeavour* put out from Plymouth Sound into the open ocean and into history on a voyage which would not only contribute to the knowledge of the known world but would change the character of English and international science for half a century.

On September 12th, the *Endeavour* made its first landfall at Madeira, where Banks collected furiously. After three days, the ship was off again, reaching Rio dè Janeiro on November 13th. There officialdom interfered with collecting, but Banks and Solander contrived to amass 315 specimens by subterfuges.

On December 7th, they were again on their way, sailing to Tierra del Fuego and around Cape Horn. The voyage was troubled by illness and suffering from the cold, but by January 20th collecting went on again. Then gradually, as the ship entered the Pacific, they returned to warmer waters and the islands of the South Seas. Tahiti was reached on April 11th, and there they stayed until July 13th, collecting, making friends with the natives (often intimate friends with the young girls), and enjoying the climate. Banks was the only member of the expedition to acquire a useful knowledge of the language, remarkable because of his lack of general linguistic ability. Captain Cook, who had been on friendly terms with Banks, recognized his remarkable ability to create trust and confidence among the natives, already demonstrated in Tierra del Fuego. This was little needed among the Tahitians but vital in the later part of the journey. Captain Cook also acknowledged his sharp eye for detail by borrowing from Banks's journal in his own account of the voyage.

It was now time to prepare for the Transit of Venus on June 2, the observations being in charge of Charles Green, the astronomer Cook had brought for the purpose. Cook ordered the building of a stockade by the River Tiapopoo, which served both as defense and source of fresh water. Despite the troublesome flies, progress went smoothly enough until it was found that the astronomical quadrant had been stolen. Banks and Green went in pursuit and recovered it bit by bit, along with other property the natives had taken. When only a few days remained before the great event, Cook set up two sub-observatories, one on the eastern part of the island, the other on a small island now called Moorea. Banks went with the latter. The evening before the transit was bright and clear, but during the night the weather became changeable and members of the party took turns in getting up every half hour to report conditions. Next morning, all was well, with clear skies and dazzling sunshine. On return to Fort Venus Banks found the company in high spirits, for the observations were more successful than anyone had dared hope.

It was not until July 13th that the *Endeavour* again set sail for the Society Islands. Banks and Solander collected whenever they could get ashore, acquiring a unique group of specimens and subjects for the artists to paint. Now it was time for Captain Cook to turn to the second set of orders, which was to confirm or prove false, once and for all, the rumors of a great southern continent. As the *Endeavour* sailed through the vast Pacific, there were apparent sightings of shores, but not until October 7th did they reach a large body of land, and then it was New Zealand and not the Great Southern Continent.

Here the expedition had a far more hostile reception from the Maoris than it had in any of its previous ports of call. New Zealand had been discovered and partially explored, but Captain Cook extended knowledge of its geography, particularly important since its large land mass could have been a part of a continent, as Banks contended for some months. The Captain discovered the passage between the North and South Islands, still known as Cook's Strait. Here the expedition had first-hand experience with cannibals, which naturally horrified the members. Such events reduced Banks's opportunities to collect, especially unfortunate because of the unique flora now known to exist there.

The *Endeavour* left New Zealand on March 31st; on April 19th the east coast of Australia appeared on the horizon. On May 1, 1770, Captain Cook, Banks, Solander, and an escort began serious exploration of the country. The natives were quite different from any they had seen before, their stark naked black bodies fantastically painted and bones piercing their noses. Banks was reaping an incredible harvest, which yielded 331 Australian plants new to European science before the expedition left. But many serious mischances beset their Australian explorations. The *Endeavour* got caught on a coral reef and was only saved by Cook's superb seamanship. Water got in the hold and many of Banks's specimens were ruined. It was the Great Barrier Reef that caused this trouble. As Lemmon states:

> Away it stretched in front of the *Endeavour's* course for 1,200 surf-girt miles, hugging the east coast and keeping within its flanking coral, which lay sometimes but ten miles or so away, sometimes ninety, some of the most dangerous shallows, sandbanks, wicked currents, flat and mountainous islands, and coral spurs, hidden and menacing and unnavigable channels ever set to catch the unwary navigator.

As the *Endeavour* pushed northward, the Great Barrier Reef continued and Cook noted in his log, "I was quite at a loss which way to steer." In this moment of peril, it was to Banks that Cook turned in the hope of forcing a channel. It speaks volumes for Banks's skill in observation, courage, and common sense that he was chosen over any sailor in the crew. Together they found a passage through which the *Endeavour* could pass and for the first time in three months they were out of sight of land. For them the Great Barrier Reef had opened. Though the passage northward still had its hazards, the worst was over. Then homeward bound.

The first stop was New Guinea for fresh food, then on to Batavia, well known as one of the most unhealthy places on earth. So it proved for the expedition. Banks, Solander, and Cook were all seriously ill, and six of the crew died, while others were so sick that they would not reach England. One was Green, the astronomer, who was thus denied the acclaim his observations on the Transit of Venus warranted. But Batavia provided the facilities for satisfactory repair of the *Endeavour* and the voyage progressed without serious problems around the Cape of Good Hope, then to St. Helena, where they made a brief stop. Banks noted that it was a good place for reconditioning plants being transported from distant parts, and so it proved to later plant hunters. From there on, it was a smooth sail with a landing at Deal at three in the afternoon on July 12, 1771.

So ended quietly a journey of 1052 days that was destined to pass into history. It had achieved its objectives — to make accurate determinations of the Transit of Venus and to prove that there was no Great Southern Continent. It had greatly improved the mapping of New Zealand and Australia, including discovery of the Great Barrier Reef, and had added immeasurably to knowledge of natural history.

No less important was its effect on Cook and Banks: 1052 days, none free from peril and many with the threat of violent death! The journey had tried them and not found them wanting. Cook left as an obscure naval officer and returned as one of the greatest figures in the voyages of discovery. Banks left as an eager amateur of botany and returned as a professional who had made enormous additions to natural science. What is more important is that the voyage proved his ability to command, his capacity to deal with people of the most varied sorts, and his acuteness of observation. It was the foundation on which he was to build a great career in a different direction and underlay all his later achievements.

So great was Banks's fame on re-entering London society that the expedition was referred to as "Mr. Banks's voyage." His personality was a major factor in such recognition, yet it included elements which seem contradictory. He was assured and dogmatic, qualities enhanced by the voyage. At the same time he was generous to a degree, making his collections freely available to scientists and amateurs alike and beginning a practice, which he would continue throughout his life, of supporting research by his own funds when there were worthy projects to be undertaken. Most of these contributions varied from £500 to £2,000. Allowing for the inflation of two centuries, these would have the purchasing power of from $75,000 to $300,000 in 1982. Banks thus became almost a private National Institute of Health in modern terms.

For one so given to command, it is surprising that he had the great gift of easy communication and enduring friendship with the most diverse people. Having demonstrated this with Captain Cook and the crew of the *Endeavour,* along with the natives of Tierra del Fuego and the South Seas, he now met King George III, who was interested in natural science and exploration. Thus began a lifelong friendship and collaboration with far-reaching results which will receive later comment.

About three years after Banks's return, Sir Joshua Reynolds painted his portrait. Banks is richly dressed in a red velvet coat trimmed with fur and a touch of lace at the throat and cuff, a symbolic globe at his side. Sir Joshua caught both sides of the personality, the dominance and the gentleness.

Banks wanted to go along on Captain Cook's second voyage, but difficulties arose after preparations were begun. His planning was, however, put to use in a brief trip to Iceland in 1772. Boswell records Dr. Johnson's intense interest in an account of that journey, for Banks later became a member of Johnson's club. This tells a good deal about both men. Of Johnson, it shows his eagerness for information, even far from his usual interests. Of Banks, it demonstrates his depth of knowledge and fluency in conversation, for Dr. Johnson was not one to tolerate the superficial or the tongue-tied.

In 1777 Banks bought a large house at 32 Soho Square, which was to be his London residence for the rest of his life. As his collections continued to grow, he built an extension and there welcomed young scientists, who were allowed to use the collections freely and who were encouraged in their careers. These included several who later became famous, including Humphrey Davy, later to succeed him in his most important position.

In 1778 Sir John Pringle resigned as president of the Royal Society. There were only two serious candidates to succeed him: Alexander Aubert, a wealthy London merchant and amateur astronomer, and Banks. The pre-election discussion centered around the type of lightning rod affording effective protection for ammunition dumps. The most effective had been invented by Benjamin Franklin, but he was now a rebel and the King's wrath was great when the Royal Society favored his design. Since the King was Patron of the Society, his support was vital and Banks, his friend, was the man most able to soothe His Majesty. The election was almost unanimous, and President of the Royal Society he remained until his death 42 years later.

This office is a position of utmost distinction. When I was in Cambridge 35 years ago, conversation would sometimes settle around the question, "If you could choose any academic position in England, which would you prefer to be, President of the Royal Society or Master of Trinity College?" The only satisfactory solution seemed to be that of Lord Adrian, who held both posts at the same time. The president in 1982 is Professor Sir Andrew Huxley, Nobel laureate and the most distinguished living member of a family whose contributions to the arts and sciences are legendary.

Now established in a high position and in a large house in Soho Square, it was time for Banks to marry. Though he had had two serious love affairs in his youth and had known the favors of the South Sea maidens, it was not until a year after his election that he married Dorothea Hugessen. The household included also Joseph's sister, Sarah Sophia, and Dr. Solander. All worked unceasingly at the great and expanding botanical collections, but the two ladies had other collections of their own. Mrs. Banks was a discriminating collector of oriental china, recognizing long before other connoisseurs that the most beautiful and desirable china was that made before contact with the West began. The sister's interests were more trivial: cartoons, visiting cards, medals, and newspaper clippings. They were a close family, and social invitations were invariably addressed to all three.

About this time John Russell made pastel portraits of the entire family.* These included Banks's mother, shown as an intelligent, kindly

---

The great-great-granddaughter of John Russell became Professor Dorothy S. Russell, for a generation the most distinguished neuropathologist in Britain and arguably in the world — an inspiration, counselor, and friend to so many.

old lady. His portrait of Joseph indicates the gentle side of his nature; it has often been reproduced. Mrs. Banks looks chubby and pleasant but not very beautiful, while the sister appears angular and gaunt.

Two years after his marriage, in 1781, he received a baronetcy, and in 1795 he was made Knight of the Bath. Now as Sir Joseph Banks, President of the Royal Society, he began a public career which was to touch many phases of science. The *Dictionary of Scientific Biography* states, "Banks dominated the scientific community of England and presided over its affairs for many years in the same way that Samuel Johnson presided over the literary community."

Banks's activities took five disparate directions, but underlying them all were the experiences of the *Endeavour* voyage. He had seen more of the world's flora than any other botanist of the time, and he could determine the regions most likely to produce valuable garden subjects or contribute to knowledge of plant life. He also knew at first hand the best methods for transporting seeds and plants through long voyages in different climates. These voyages were full of danger, as he also knew. For Cook and Banks the Great Barrier Reef had been crossed by virtue of superb seamanship and luck, but for three-quarters of Banks's plant hunters the catastrophes were not surmounted. Yet he did not ask them to take chances which he had not dared himself.

His stop in South Africa had impressed him with the richness of its flora, and there he sent his first plant hunter, Masson, who brought back hundreds of new species, which now enrich gardens and greenhouses. Then there was Menzies, who Banks sent to the Americas. His most notable introductions were the giant redwood and the monkey puzzle tree, now a familiar, if questionable, addition to English gardens.

Banks was interested in Chinese plants, then known only by rumor in England and jealously guarded by the Chinese. He utilized several men there on diplomatic missions, but in 1806 he was able to send out a professional collector, William Kerr, who introduced many valuable garden subjects. This indicates Sir Joseph's method of directing plant explorations, but there were many others to Russia, Iceland, India, and elsewhere.

By far the most familiar of the expeditions directed by Banks was that designed to introduce the breadfruit tree of the South Seas into the West Indies as a source of cheap food. He chose Captain William Bligh as captain of the *Bounty*, with the result of the famous mutiny and Bligh's incredible journey of 3,618 miles in an open boat. Movies have depicted Bligh as a cruel monster, but movies are an unreliable source of history. The only evidence that Bligh was cruel is the testimony of men on trial for their lives when they knew their statements could not be verified. Bligh's problem seemed to be that he had a rigid disposition and believed that orders were orders, to be obeyed. Regardless of the crew's protests, the breadfruit trees had the deck space the crew expected for themselves and received fresh water whether there was any for the men or not. There is also the suggestion that the mutineers were reluctant to exchange the gentle climate and accessible maidens of Tahiti for English weather and society. At any rate, Sir Joseph, no mean judge of men, selected Captain Bligh for a second attempt, which was successful. The breadfruit trees proved easy to propagate and flourish there to this day. Bligh remained in the navy and was a Vice Admiral at the time of his retirement.

The second direction of Sir Joseph's activities was the establishment of a center where these diverse plants could be grown and studied. His opportunity for this effort depended on his friendship with the King, which was one more result of the *Endeavour* voyage.

This he did at Kew, where George III's mother, Augusta, Princess of Wales, had established a botanic garden more or less along the lines of those in modern cities, including Chicago. Banks was the moving force in transforming Kew into a great institution of scientific botany and a place where the plant introductions could be grown and living material, in contrast to his own herbarium, made available to gardeners and scientists. Sir Joseph did not hold the title of Director of Kew, but was that unofficially, starting it on its way to its present position as the greatest institution of its kind in the world.

The third direction Sir Joseph took was the improvement of agriculture, an interest shared with the King, who came to be known as "Farmer George." Banks loved his Lincolnshire estates and spent three months each year at Revesby. He participated in the local activities and had a part in the Lincolnshire Riots of 1796. New methods of agriculture and animal husbandry were encouraged. The King was interested in bringing merino sheep from Spain to improve English wool. These sheep, however, were jealously guarded by the Spanish and sales to foreigners forbidden by law. Banks was entrusted with the delicate diplomatic task of obtaining them for England, a major accomplishment.

The fourth thrust of Sir Joseph's energy was toward the societies which were being formed as scientific advances in many fields made them necessary. Banks's interest was two-fold: promotion of scientific interchange and protection of the Royal Society from domination by any other organization. The Horticultural Society (now the Royal Horticultural Society) he welcomed warmly and contributed to its journal. His reception of the Royal Institution was less cordial, though not hostile, because it was more likely to compete with the Royal Society. In the same way, he nurtured many scientific societies but declined to take part in those devoted to art and letters, pleading lack of ability. Perhaps unconsciously he realized that they posed no threat to the Royal Society. It was, however, his work with organizations that established his dominance in the science of his time.

The fifth, and crowning, activity was encouragement of scientific interchange internationally. Delays as long as twenty years often occurred in transmitting knowledge of scientific advances between France and England. Now the situation was much worse because the two nations were at war, but Sir Joseph's influence was such that even that obstacle was surmounted. A letter of March 18, 1797, to M. Charretie expresses his attitude:

> Sir — I lose not a moment in returning to you my best thanks for the zealous and effectual steps you have taken to open an intercourse between the *Institut National* and the Royal Society. Such communication cannot but be of material use to the progress of Science; and may also lay the foundation of a better understanding between the two countries in future than, unfortunately for both, has of late years taken place. . . .

Sir Joseph was also often able by his international connections to secure the release of scientists who had become prisoners of war. When he failed, he could sometimes obtain more favorable treatment for the prisoners, and he even arranged for the cargoes of ships on scientific expeditions to be released to French ports. Banks had been impressed by Benjamin Franklin's protection of Captain Cook on his voyages during the American Revolution, and he carried this sort of protection much farther.

Gradually, years and illness overtook this many-faceted man, but he persisted in the face of gout and diminishing physical strength. He eventually sent a resignation to the Royal Society, but this was not accepted. President he remained even when he had to be carried to the Chair. He last presided only three months before his death. In the 42 years of Sir Joseph's presidency there were 450 meetings, and he presided over 417 of them.

Death came quietly on June 19, 1820, in the same year it came to George III, his friend and patron. At his own request, there was no funeral pomp and no stone or tablet marks his grave.

In view of Banks's dominant position in eighteenth-century England, it is surprising that writings about him are sparse and usually superficial. There are reasons for this. Banks wrote no large work, his bibliography consisting of only 20 short notes on horticultural and agricultural subjects. He and Solander had nearly completed an edition of the detailed *Endeavour* journal at the time of Solander's death in 1782. Sir Joseph, occupied with the affairs of the Royal Society, put it aside for the moment, but the moment was a long one. A definitive edition only appeared in 1962, 180 years later, and a facsimile edition with reproductions of the drawings in 1980, 198 years after the "moment" began.

Over 800 letters of Banks exist, but these tell little of the man. His handwriting was so illegible that he employed an amanuensis for nearly all. Most are written in the third person and dealt with business of the Royal Society, only half a dozen having any personal references at all.

Most tragic of all is the fate of the Banks papers, though the collections are safe in the British Museum (Natural History). The papers were deposited on indefinite loan in the British Museum. Title to them passed to Lord Brabourne in 1882. He repossessed them and had them auctioned at Sotheby's, where they brought only £182 19s. Many were bought by autograph dealers and the rest scattered in Australia, New Zealand, Canada, and the United States, as well as

England. So the stroke of the auctioneer's gavel dispersed the record of a distinguished lifetime to the ends of the earth.

To write a definitive biography of Banks would entail special requirements. The author would need to have literary skill, a professional knowledge of botany, command of eighteenth-century social and scientific history, familiarity with the sea and the voyages of discovery, as well as facility for world travel. That person has not yet appeared. Meanwhile, we must evaluate his contributions as best we can.

Sir Humphrey Davy, who followed Banks as President of the Royal Society after a temporary chairmanship, commented:

> He was a good-humoured and liberal man, free and various in conversational power, a tolerable botanist, and generally acquainted with Natural History. He had not much reading, and no profound information. He was always ready to promote the objects of men of science, but he required to be regarded as a patron, and readily swallowed gross flattery. When he gave anecdotes of his voyages he was very entertaining and unaffected. A courtier in character, he was a warm friend to a good King. In his relations to the Royal Society he was too personal, and made his house a circle too like a Court.

That, from a man whose career Banks had nurtured and who now held the position Banks had done so much to dignify. It recalls a remark of Lucien Guitry, "Does someone bore you? Do him a favor and you will soon see no more of him."

In sharp contrast, Lyte, Banks's recent biographer, states that Banks would "lift science out of the alchemists' den and plant it firmly in the laboratory." This is far too much. That change did indeed occur during Banks's lifetime, but it resulted from the work of many scientists in France, Germany, Sweden, and elsewhere, as well as in England. If I were to choose one man most responsible for this achievement, it would be Lavoisier, but that would be unfair because change was due to discoveries of many scholars in many disciplines.

It is more revealing to compare Banks's activities with those of a symphony conductor. All great conductors can play one or more instruments, often at highly proficient levels, but seldom, if ever, is the same person equally famous as conductor and solo virtuoso. So Banks was a learned botanist, probably as proficient as any in England at that time but not at all the equal of his Swedish contemporary Linnaeus or of the later directors of Kew, Sir William and Sir Joseph Hooker, or of their American contemporary, Asa Gray. What the symphony conductor does is to cue first the strings, then the woodwinds, then the brasses so as to create a whole which is the vision of the composer. So, too, Banks sent out plant collectors now to South Africa, then to the Orient, then to America, with the result that botany and horticulture expanded more rapidly than in any other equivalent period of years. The symphony conductor will sometimes turn to opera, where he must fuse orchestra, voices, and dramatic action in just proportions, while giving the star singers due prominence. So Banks turned to learned organizations, but always he was careful to keep the star, the Royal Society, in the leading position. Finally, the symphony conductor may take his orchestra to other countries, promoting international exchange in music. So Banks sponsored and promoted the sharing of results and ideas in many countries, even under the most adverse conditions. That achievement of Banks has proved permanent. Though sometimes sullied, internationalism remains the ideal, the guiding light, in the arts and sciences.

PART TWO

Portraits of Villainy

Mordre wol out, certeyn, it wol nat faille.

GEOFFREY CHAUCER, THE PRIORESS'S TALE
(1369)

CHAPTER FIVE

Delight in Evil

~

THERE IS A FAMILIAR REMARK that detective fiction is the last refuge of the intellectual. Examples of such experts in the art known to me are L.J. Henderson, the physicochemical biologist; Shields Warren, authority on radiation and early member of the Atomic Energy Commission; D.S. Russell, perhaps the greatest living neuropathologist. The learning of President F.D. Roosevelt in this field of fiction is well known. In seeking a common denomination for so diverse a group, I offer the hypothesis that it may be found in chronic insomnia. It is amazing how easily one goes off to untroubled sleep while the heroine is clinging to the top of a thousand-foot cliff, with the villain pounding on her knuckles. The variation from one's own life experience is so great and the implausabilities are so frequent that there is no emotional involvement, only the flow of none-too-distinguished prose.

But after a time detective fiction loses its value as a soporific. The situations become too expected, the writing formulae too obvious and mechanical. The writers are constrained by the requirements of possibility, improbable though they may be. It is at this point that true crime writing takes over — but true crime reporting

Read at the Chicago Literary Club on March 25, 1968.

of a specific type. There is no interest beyond the daily newspaper in a description of stabbings, shootings, and the latest doings of Gangsterland. Violence in itself is unattractive and too abundant at all periods of history to engage much interest. But there are, at most diverse times and places, examples of ingenious wickedness in the human race, which become footnotes to social history and which are far too improbable to be permitted the writers of detective fiction.

Take, for instance, the domestic duck as an instrument of justice. In July 1897 there was a man who raised ducks in Woodside, Long Island — ordinary, white ducks destined for the oven in fall and winter. But one day a fine white bird named Julia left for her daily explorations and returned strangely changed, for her breast was now crimson, and not from reflections of the sunset. Her owner, curious about this transformation, followed her next day and soon saw her happily swimming in a pool he had never seen before, and the water was as crimson as Julia's breast. In the end, it turned out that this was only the final link in a chain of strange implausabilities. Mrs. Nack and her lover, Mr. Thorn, decided to get rid of the former's other lover, Willie Guldensuppe. So they did, and dismembered his body in the bathtub. To get rid of the blood, Thorn left the tap running for a couple of days; it was estimated that 40,000 gallons of water dissolved Willie's blood. The couple congratulated themselves on getting rid of all the telltale crimson in the sewers. But what they did not know was that there were no sewers in Woodside. The 40,000 gallons made a great pool outside the cottage, and then came Julia, the Avenging Angel in guise of a duck. Thorn was executed but Mrs. Nack got off with nine years for manslaughter.

But this brief history by no means concludes the role of the domestic duck in criminal investigation. At Doylestown, Pennsylvania, in the February term of court in 1832, an appropriately named lady,

Lucretia Chapman, and her lover, Nino Amalia Espos y Mina, were jointly tried for poisoning Mr. Chapman. Espos was convicted but, as is the way with lady poisoners, Lucretia escaped unscathed — a phenomenon of which some further account will be given. None of this might have come to light had not one of the neighbors, Benjamin Butcher by name, kept a flock of ducks. I quote from Mr. Butcher's testimony relating to the events of Tuesday, June 21, 1831, when he saw his ducks returning from the Chapmans' yard on which they were wont to trespass:

> They seemed to be worried. They walked in a row, one after the other. Before the ducks came through into the road one of them fell over dead. The rest came through the fence where the waste water emptied and then another fell over. When they got nearly across the road a third fell over. One of my boys came out and I told him to take care of the ducks; I went in the shop. After a little the boy came and said another was dead, and he thought they would all die. I told him to bury them. There were between twenty and thirty died that day and the next. Four of the ducks could not get through into Mr. Chapman's yard; these did not die. . . . I heard that Mr. Chapman had cholera morbus.

Thus it came out that arsenic was in the discarded chicken soup, the fat was in the fire, and a flock of ducks were responsible for revealing that which had been hidden. No, the duck as agent in criminal investigation is far too improbable for the detective novelist, but in fact it may on occasion fill this role quite well.

What makes a crime sufficiently memorable to engage the sustained interest and talents of gifted writers? Suitable cases are not common. So far, we have ruled out overt and everyday violence and ruled in the improbability which truth has and which is denied to fiction. But there are other criteria. One is that the murder should have been committed by a person of otherwise blameless life and preferably by a person of education and of middle class. He is thus most vulnerable to, and conscious of, the opinions of those about him. He also has the incentive for ingenious concealment and, one would expect, the intelligence to carry it out. But in that supposition we are wrong. Ingenious such a murderer may be, but he is so often undone precisely by his own cleverness. Therein lies the peculiar charm of many of these crimes. As has been said, "The ineptitude of the experts is inexplicable." For instance, among classic crimes there are several examples of physicians who seemed to go out of their way to select the very poisons which are most easily traced. Then, too, an old murder is better than a new one, for the strange circumstances of the crime are enhanced by remoteness of time and setting.

Some murders derive a special interest from the fact that, once the deed has been accomplished, the murderer finds himself with an unwanted corpse on his hands, and his efforts to rid himself of this human albatross may be as picturesque as they are desperate. Therein may lie part of the explanation for the fact that the number of notable crimes in Britain is out of proportion to its low homicide rate. Few parts of that small and populous country are so seldom visited as to allow gross dumping of corpses without assurance of prompt discovery. Consider the Londoner John George Haigh, who exchanged a good upbringing and honest life in the 1930s for various smaller criminous pursuits and in the 1940s for a series of profitable murders — nine according to his account, probably exaggerated. He was successful in ridding himself of his victims by the simple expedient of dissolving them in sulphuric acid — successful, that is, until

1949, when various strange and traceable objects were found in the acid bath of an obscure laboratory, including intact full upper and lower dentures.

Once identified, a single telling does not by any means exhaust the possibilities of a fine murder. The most conscientious of writers have produced as many as three essays on the same case and different authors have freely used one anothers' cases, but each essay is interesting and valid in its own right. For this reason, I make no apologies for using illustrations well known to all. The same vineyard produces many vintages from the same grapes, each different and of varying excellence, but all interesting.

It has been said with some truth that Edgar Allen Poe's claim to be the originator of detective fiction rests on an output of four short stories, all that can be accepted as such among the many he wrote, but that each is of a different type and that no genuinely original basic pattern has since emerged. So, too, there is a definite starting point in true crime writing. In 1827 T. De Quincy wrote an essay and in 1839 and 1854 produced supplementary papers which are actually appendices. De Quincy's essay has been hailed for 140 years as a classic more often than it is read. As G.K. Chesterton pointed out, "A classic is a book which we praise without reading." For evidence of this neglect in fact and regard on paper, it is not necessary to look beyond De Quincy's title, which is nearly always misquoted. For the record, it is, "On Murder Considered as One of the Fine Arts." At once, De Quincy states the viewpoint, "Murder, for instance, may be laid hold of by its moral handle (as it generally is in the pulpit, and at the Old Bailey), and *that,* I confess, is its weak side; or it may also be treated aesthetically, as the Germans call it — that is, in relation to good taste." He was rather more attracted by crimes of overt violence than most of his followers have been, but he much preferred the murder of philosophers to that of princes, which is to say political assassinations. De Quincy's essay has the charm of an excellent but now outmoded style. He must be considered one of the first in rank, as well as in time, as a portrayer of curious misdeeds.

The qualifications of a fine practitioner of the art of classic crime writing are quite special. He must have a thorough literary background and be able to call upon a clear and graceful style of writing. It is well for him to be a successful collector of odd and ancient books and pamphlets. But far beyond these is the requirement that he have a deep understanding of human personality and motivation, with a pleasure in the quirks of the people whom he is interpreting. The lightness of presentation can never fail for a moment with impunity. If you like, he must have an unwavering delight in evil. To illustrate this, I choose a passage from William Roughead, perhaps the greatest writer in the genre and to whom, along with his friend and colleague, Edmund Pearson, the rest of this essay will be devoted. Here is Mr. Roughead delighting in evil:

> In the Glasgow of the early sixties the Sandyford Mystery (with a capital *M*) was the topic not only of the hour, but of the year. The Second City, in mid-Victorian times, was singularly rich in wrongdoers of the most attaching type. There was the wonderful Miss Madeleine Smith in 1857, there was the poisonous Dr. Pritchard in 1865; and between these twain, in 1862, a first-class case, bristling with sensation and strange surprises, possessing everything requisite to a great criminal drama and constituting, in my submission, an ideal murder. For to do one's self the deed of which by means of your evidence another is

convicted, is a veritable triumph of naughtiness only to be com-
passed by a past-master of the art of homicide.

Such is the spirit of delight in evil. William Roughead, a Scotsman born in 1870, was educated at Edinburgh University, admitted a
member of the Society of Writers to His Majesty's Signet in 1893, and
a Scotsman at heart until his death in 1952. As a young lawyer, he
would from time to time wander into the court where murder trials
happened to be in progress. Quite soon he began to take an interest
which was as much literary as legal. Mr. Roughead speaks thus of his
discovery:

> Murder has a magic of its own, its peculiar alchemy. Touched
> by that crimson wand things base and sordid, things ugly and of
> ill report, are transformed into matters wondrous, weird and
> tragical. Dull streets become fraught with mystery, common-
> place dwellings assume a sinister aspect, everyone concerned,
> howsoever plain and ordinary, is invested with a new value and
> importance as the red light falls upon each. The moveless figure
> in the dock, the passing cloud of witnesses, even the poor and
> pitiful exhibits, all are endowed with a different character and
> hold for a space the popular attention, ere they revert once again
> to their customary and homely selves.

Besides his own essays, Roughead early had the opportunity to
write some prefaces for the *Notable British Trials* series, an important
step upward which he reciprocated by lending new luster to that distinguished publication. A few of these were trials which he had himself attended, and he could bring a rare immediacy to his accounts.

In fact, Roughead was so much the Scotsman that (at least to this reader) his accounts of Scottish crimes were better than those of crimes which took place south of the Border, on the Continent, occasionally in the United States, and rarely in Ireland.

Roughead gives another reason why some Scottish trials have a special character when they end in the uniquely Scottish verdict of "Not Proven." As he says, "The indeterminate verdict, Not Proven, leaves unanswered the question at issue, and furnishes the student of such matters with a problem that defies solution." Later he cites with qualified approval the remark that Not Proven really means "Not guilty — but don't do it again."

Now a true and just account of any trial involves three separate parts: fact, interpretation, and surmise. It is perhaps a result of legal training, but also of clear thinking and meticulous study, that Roughead keeps these so separate that even the most careless reader cannot misconstrue them. The facts are carefully weighed, the interpretation is judicious, and the surmise, if any is given, is cogent and responsible.

In fact, his surmise in one preface in *Notable British Trials* had far-reaching results. This was the first trial of Oscar Slater of Glasgow in 1909. He was well equipped to be the historian, for he had attended the trial, knew the location, and was acquainted with some of those involved. Slater was accused of the murder of an 83-year-old solitary and isolated woman, Miss Marion Gilchrist, notable among others of her kind only in that she kept £3,000 worth of jewels in her wardrobe. The intricacies of this case, more procedural than factual, would require several writings. In brief, the old lady's jewels were scattered about when her body was found, but her maid declared that a diamond brooch was missing. Eventually, the police turned up a neighbor, Oscar Slater, whose sole values as a suspect were two:

that he was trying to dispose of a pawn ticket for a diamond brooch, which soon was shown not to be Miss Gilchrist's at all and had been in continuous pawn for over a month before the murder; and second, that he had openly left Glasgow to return to America, according to a prearranged plan. On such flimsy evidence and in view of some manipulations within the police force, Slater was convicted of murder and sentenced to death, later commuted to life imprisonment. The reason for citing this curious case, however, is that Roughead's eyewitness account of the trial appeared in *Notable British Trials,* with all its carefully separated fact, interpretation, and gentle but devastating surmise. This came to the attention of Sir Arthur Conan Doyle, who decided that the Roughead surmise demanded that something be done in the cause of justice. Questions were asked of the Scottish Secretary in the House of Commons, others helped and five years later, in 1914, there was an official inquiry, which Roughead describes as "Gilbertian"; it left matters wholly unchanged. Only in 1928 was the case retried by the Scottish Court of Criminal Appeal. Slater's legal advisers had a major problem in reassembling witnesses to events nearly 20 years old. Mrs. Gilchrist's maid, for instance, was living peacefully in Peoria and refused to return. However, sufficient evidence was secured with the help of such experts as Sir Bernard Spilsbury to obtain an acquittal after Slater had spent nineteen years in prison.

The Slater case is a notable one in the annals of justice, but it is too full of legal intricacies and bickerings within the halls of justice to qualify it as a shining example of crime for the connoisseur. On the other hand, it occupies a very special niche in that literature because it demonstrates that the marshalling of fact, interpretation, and surmise in the hands of a wise and literate master may have on occasion a practical result without losing the light touch, the delight in evil, even though the evil is not the prisoner's but largely that of the system in which he finds himself entangled.

It is time to turn to Mr. Roughead's treatment of perhaps the most classic of all crimes, those of Burke and Hare, who graced the city of Edinburgh with their presence in the 1820s. These experts in filling their pockets at the cost of the lives of various waifs and strays are well known. They were famous long before Roughead was born and their antics had long since brought about changes in the laws governing anatomical dissection. But, as I have said, a choice crime is worthy of many accounts, and murderers as picturesque as Burke and Hare deserve to be recalled again and again, for they are historical figures passing into legend. Certainly Roughead thought so, for three essays by him are known to me, and my survey is far from complete.

As you will recall, Hare assisted the widow Log to carry on the business of a tramps' hostel in Tanner's Close, a wretched cul-de-sac in West Port near the site of the old gates in the Edinburgh wall, long since vanished. There came to live at the hostel one William Burke, a laborer who shared with Hare a taste for potatoes and whiskey. On November 29, 1927, when funds for this simple diet were low, an elderly inmate of the hostel died, owing £4. It seemed only justice to recover the debt by selling the body for anatomical dissection. Such subjects were greatly in demand at Edinburgh, because two rival professors of anatomy, Drs. Monro and Knox, were active dissectors and competitors. As Roughead puts it:

> In order to supply the constant and increasing demand for "subjects," there had grown up an ancillary branch of research, carried out behind the scenes by the professional riflers of graves, known by the expressive names of Body Snatchers or

Resurrectionists. These subordinate ministers to the needs of science were by the nature of their calling persons of irregular and often drunken habits, as unreliable as they were greedy and unscrupulous, so it frequently happened that the students themselves had to do their own catering, lest the "table" of the "Chief" should lack its daily indispensible equipment.

Thus it was with some relief that a student of Dr. Knox directed Burke and Hare to his own establishment instead of that presided over by Professor Monro, where they had intended to offer their wares. The body was approved by Dr. Knox himself, and Burke and Hare left £7 10s richer. As this fine pair meditated on their affluence, a great idea struck them. Why wait for another inmate of the hostel to leave this world to their profit? The process could be accelerated simply by a little assistance, especially to the old and friendless, to whom life was at best a burden.

This idea proved unexpectedly easy to put into execution (pun strictly intended) and their coffers swelled. Since the top price of £10 was regularly paid for such fresh material, Burke each time received £4, Hare £5, and the Widow Log (or Mrs. Hare, as she called herself) £1, as a sort of gratuity. It is not quite certain how many times they repeated this procedure, for Burke and Hare even became confused themselves, but it was often enough to improve the household finances to a degree readily noted by the neighbors.

Success engendered boldness and caution was finally thrown to the winds on April 9, 1828, when they chose for their attentions a beautiful 18-year-old prostitute, Mary Patterson. Mary and her friend, Janet Brown, were lured to the hostel and given many drinks, which brought the hoped-for oblivion to Mary but not to Janet, whose flight was promoted by an argument with Burke's current mistress. But Mary turned up on the dissecting table of Dr. Knox, who was charmed by her beauty as much as by her anatomical freshness. But Mr. Fergusson, the assistant, knew Mary and named her. This gentleman later became a baronet and Surgeon to that model of middle class morality, the late Queen Victoria. But then he was only a humble assistant and accepted Burke's feeble explanations.

So Burke and Hare continued to minister to the unfortunate in their own fashion and on an increasing scale. Among those receiving attention were a dumb boy, Daft Jamie, and his grandmother; even Burke's conscience revolted after this one. So successful was the business that a regular arrangement was made with Dr. Knox: £10 in winter, £8 in summer, cash on delivery. Curiously enough for all their carelessness, the final murder was in the original pattern: that of Mrs. Docherty, a poor little old beggar woman on Halloween of 1828. Some guests at the holiday celebration missed the old lady and chanced upon the body by looking in a forbidden corner when Burke was out for more whiskey. Police were summoned and the pair and Burke's mistress were brought to the dock.

Hare eagerly turned King's Evidence when approached by the Lord Advocate. The trial was to be for the murder of Mrs. Docherty, a fortunate choice for Dr. Knox, for hers was the only body he had not personally inspected. Thus he escaped giving evidence, but his reputation was ruined and he pursued a steadily downhill path for 38 years, one of his last occupations being demonstrator of a traveling party of Ojibbeway Indians. But he did get mention in a popular quatrain:

> *Up the close and down the stair,*
> *But and ben wi' Burke and Hare.*
> *Burke's the butcher, Hare's the thief,*
> *Knox the boy that buys the beef. . . .*

Burke's mistress was acquitted and passes from history. Hare, as King's Evidence, was released and promptly traveled south by the mail coach in disguise. At the very first stop he was recognized, beset by an angry mob, and given refuge in prison. Early next morning he was escorted by militiamen beyond the border, and nothing certain is known after that. There is a tradition that he was cast into a lime pit by fellow workers who recognized him and, thus losing his vision, he lived on for many years as a blind beggar in the streets of London.

Perhaps Burke's fate was more merciful. He was sentenced to be hanged, his body publicly dissected, and his skeleton preserved in the Museum. All this was duly carried out on January 29, 1829.

In September 1967 I paid visits to the museums of the Anatomy Department of Edinburgh University and of the Royal College of Surgeons of Edinburgh, of which each possess relics of this notable pair. Both were opened for me very kindly on a day which proved to be a Scottish holiday. There I saw Burke's skeleton and can give eyewitness evidence to the truth of the rumor that Burke's vertebrae did not fracture at the drop, so he was well and truly strangled. Casts of the two faces suggest Burke as the stronger character, as indeed he behaved. Burke's body was also flayed and the skin tanned. On display was a grisly relic, a pocketbook made from Burke's skin, after 139 years a little fragmented but otherwise much like my own. Bits of the skin were also sold to souvenir collectors, one of which came to Roughead by inheritance from his grandfather, the original purchaser. He thus had a most intimate connection with the case, but all of us have some, for the legislative bodies were shocked into passing modern laws on anatomical dissection and the profitable trade of Burke and Hare ceased to be an occupation.

The gentle urbanity, concealed wit, and understanding of people which lie in Roughead's essays suggest that he would have been among the most clubbable of men. The roster of his friends confirms this, including Sir Henry Irving, Sir Max Beerbohm Tree, and Hugh Walpole. An especially warm and admiring one was Henry James. Among several published letters of James, the young Roughead must have valued this one: "Keep on with them all, please, and continue to beckon me along the gallery that I can't tread alone and where, by your leave, I link my arm fraternally in yours, the gallery of sinister perspective just stretches in this manner straight away."

But there was one friend of long standing who is more immediately connected with this essay: his American colleague and counterpart, Edmund Pearson. Though both were international figures, Pearson remained as much a New Englander at heart as ever did Roughead a Scotsman.

Pearson was born in 1880 of old New England stock in Newburyport, Massachusetts, a town whose High Street is still lined with sea captains' houses set in beautiful green lawns. After being graduated from Harvard, he left New England in body, if not in spirit, for a career as librarian in Albany, Washington, and New York, where he died at age 57. While he was born ten years after Roughead, he predeceased him by fifteen. In a scholarly essay, Miriam Allen De Ford has this to say of Pearson:

> In New York he was known as a wit and a raconteur, celebrated for his urbanity and respected for his forthright adherence to his deep-seated beliefs. People spoke in one breath of his kindness and consideration and of his scholarly, unobtrusive fund of erudition. . . .
>
> That is why in his own writing there is the patient building up of evidence, the search for the logical solution, the ambient play of dry humor, but little or no emotion . . . yet he dealt with

some of the bloodiest and most sordid affairs of criminous history. It is significant that contemporary critics compared him not with other writers on crime but with brilliant historians like Gamaliel Bradford and Lytton Strachy.

Pearson's photograph shows features hewn straight from New England granite, only a little softened by a life of letters. The corpus of his writings in the field of crime (for he wrote also other books and a regular column in the *Boston Transcript*) is composed of a book and several essays on Lizzie Borden, whose strange behavior was his abiding interest; accounts of classic crimes collected from many countries and many centuries; and a few studies with generalization.

Of the last, I have been especially struck by the one entitled *Rules for Murderesses.* Summary of this masterpiece is in itself a crime. I quote the opening statement and the rules, and a brief comment on each:

"A woman with fair opportunities," said Thackery, "and without an absolute hump, may marry whom she likes."

That is an understatement. A woman's privileges are even greater — for if she will observe a few restrictions she may *murder* whom she likes. It is three to one she will go scot-free. If she is treated with severity it is because she has disregarded one of the obvious rules. . . . She overrides these at her peril. Briefly, the regulations are as follows:

1. *If you decide to murder your husband, you must never act in concert with a lover.*
In comment upon this rule, it must be added that a lover should appear nowhere in the record: not a sign, not a suspi-

cion, not even a shoelace of his. The careful murderess of her husband removes him, unaided, and then proceeds, helped by a clever lawyer, to blacken the dead man's character. This is always successful, and very popular; she usually becomes a heroine. . . .

2. *It is inadvisable for a maidservant to murder her mistress under circumstances of extreme barbarity.*

In England, Kate Webster, about fifty years ago, killed her mistress for the purpose of robbery. . . . Webster was heard by the neighbors pounding and chopping, and was afterwards known to be boiling something in the copper washboiler. . . . Thereafter, throughout Great Britain, Kate Webster was regarded with considerable distaste, and this never ceased nor diminished until the sentence of the law was executed.

Webster blundered at every opportunity. She made the mistake of operating in England, instead of America, and of limiting her murders to one. . . . A woman's immunity from severe punishment increases according to the number of persons she murders.

3. *Even in the murder of a father or mother, the astute murderess will take care that no lover appears upon the scene.*

Plain murder is often forgiven by a jury, but murder combined with a love affair is almost always disapproved. The feeling is that somebody has been having too much fun. . . .

4. *If you commit murder for insurance money, or for mere pleasure, make it wholesale. Never stop at one.*

This regulation bears with equal force against men; women are not especially restricted at this point. The person who kills some one obscure individual, who does it quietly and with moderate civility, is in a rather perilous position. Perilous, that is, for a murderer. There are about three chances in a hundred that he may be executed.

It is the wholesale poisoner, or the shockingly cruel and unusual murderer, who attracts the sob sisters and sob brothers of the yellow press; causes quack alienists to rally to his defense like buzzards around a carcass; invites the windiest oratory and the most unmitigated flapdoodle from his attorneys; and finally, if he be convicted at all, makes thousands of persons move heaven and earth, slander the living and vilify the dead, in order to save his precious body alive.

There is lightness in this irony but also bitterness when the goings-on pass beyond the point a New England Brahmin's conscience will allow. And certainly it is permitted to hear faintly in the background the swish of the skirts of the Lady from Fall River. Lizzie Borden, if murderess she was, observed each of these rules, and it is not too much to say that the rules were formulated on her success, for Pearson was convinced that she and she alone gave her mother "forty whacks and her father forty-one." Lizzie did not act in concert with a lover and could not be shown to have one (Rules 1 and 3). She was not a maidservant but the mistress of the house, and the maidservant proved an invaluable ally (Rule 2). But it is especially Rule 4 which applies. There were two shockingly brutal murders, on which days and weeks of legal flapdoodle were expended; seldom, if ever, have sob sisters and sob brothers had a greater field day, and slanders of those living and dead at that time continue even to this day.

Pearson became obsessed with Lizzie Borden and devoted essays to her, such as the delightful "Legends of Lizzie," and a large book. In the end, he was not only convinced of Lizzie's guilt but could no longer keep his delight in her evil in its required place. It really seemed to him that it was quite naughty of Lizzie first to take an ax to her stepmother and then to her father. His New England sense of duty compelled him to attempt to convince posterity that Lizzie should not be romanticized but condemned for an ogress. It is unfair to Pearson to judge him too harshly on this one lapse from the literary canons under which he was writing. Especially is it un-justified to state that Pearson consciously selected the facts against Lizzie and suppressed those in her favor, as Radin has done. But Pearson judged and Roughead, lawyer-litterateur as he was, never did. By so much is Roughead the greater practitioner of a fragile art.

The bare outline of facts about what occurred on that scorching hot fourth of August in 1892 in a plain little two-story cottage on Second Street is simple enough when stripped of verbiage, specula-tion (acrimonious or otherwise), and legend. The inhabitants of the house at that time were normally Mr. and Mrs. Borden, their daugh-ters, Emma and Lizzie, a servant, Bridget Sullivan, and a guest, Mr. John Vinnicum Morse, brother of Mr. Borden's first wife. Now, Miss Emma was out of town on a visit, Mr. Morse was about his business in Fall River, and Mr. Bordon was also on his usual rounds. As the hot dawn waxed into torrid morning, somebody — and only Lizzie and Bridget were in the house — killed Mrs. Borden by repeated, savage blows from an ax violent enough to cave in her skull. When Mr. Borden returned at lunch time an hour and a half to two hours later, somebody gave him the same treatment while Lizzie, by her own testimony, was only 30 or 40 feet away. Mrs. Borden was mak-ing her bed when Nemesis struck, while Mr. Borden's came while he was napping on the couch downstairs.

There were some additional facts. Three witnesses testified that

Lizzie had tried to buy prussic acid at a drug store the week before, but their testimony was excluded by the court. No doubt also attaches to the fact that she burned a dress three days after the murders, very like the dress she wore on the fourth of August.

But almost at that very point, fact ceases and elaboration begins. Lizzie herself gave it a start by telling half a dozen conflicting stories before her tardy arrest, all excluded by the court to Lizzie's great benefit. Victoria Lincoln's stimulating book, "A Private Disgrace," published in 1967, has this to say after careful study of primary sources, "As a liar, Lizzie was phenomenally dull. One can scarcely overstate her supernal power to bore. And, by a remarkable paradox, it is through this lethal dullness that she provides a singular excitement: She explains the whole *modus operandi* of the crime."

The police work left something to be desired, two of the most important exhibits disappearing while in the court, among other slight irregularities; the charge to the jury was as near a direction for acquittal as makes no difference. Lizzie left the court officially declared not guilty, only to be tried fairly, unfairly, ironically, and even humorously for all these seventy-five years. Why? The reasons have best been given by Mr. Pearson himself:

> . . . In the first place it was a mysterious crime in a class of society where such deeds of violence are not only foreign but usually wildly impossible. It was purely a problem in murder, not complicated by scandals of the kind which lead to the *crime passionel,* nor by any of the circumstances of the political assassination. The evidence was wholly circumstantial. The perpetrator of the double murder was protected by a series of chances which might not happen again in a thousand years.

But these reasons alone, compelling though they are, do not suffice to explain the Fall River legend and its passage into American folklore. It seems to me that two questions and one fact are largely responsible. The fact is that carefully documented materials gathered at the time are remarkably scant, while at the same time the torrent of misinformation, sob sister distortions, and flimsy speculations at once began and have not yet been stemmed.

The first question is: If Lizzie murdered her parents, what possessed Lizzie? In an environment where custom is all and respectability the ultimate, why did she so suddenly repudiate the only pattern of life she had known that hot August morning? It has been suggested that Lizzie's acknowledged resentment against her stepmother may have suddenly burst into murderous rage, and that hatred for her father for marrying her stepmother may have made him the second victim. This is not very sound, in my opinion. The break with her whole previous behavior is too great. There is at least one more probable motive. Lizzie inherited by the two deaths half of her father's half-million dollar estate. All her actions after acquittal confirm her aspirations to rise in social class. She at once bought Maplecroft, a much more spacious house and lived grandly, at least for Fall River. And she could not bring herself to leave that place, even though few would have anything to do with her and though she never was again accepted until her death in 1927, 35 years after the great day. Is not Lizzie's desire for opulence, denied by her family when they could well afford it, enough to give a fragment of plausibility to the implausible situation? There was never a doubt that Lizzie had an iron will, both by repute and by recorded behavior. Such iron will plus the urge for respectability is a dangerous combination. Therein Lizzie again qualifies for the role of murderess:

Whoever did the deed must have had need of iron nerve in the hour and a half between the two moments of action.

The second question is: What are the alternatives? Only Bridget and Lizzie were in the house. The unidentified stranger is too mythical for serious consideration. Radin believes that Bridget went berserk and did the whole business alone, but this is improbable in the extreme. Neither before nor after was there any evidence of behavior incompatible with that of a stolid, none-too-bright, Irish servant.

Gross and, more recently, Victoria Lincoln have an alternative which is far more satisfactory: that Lizzie did the deeds alone but with the knowledge and willing consent of Bridget, for which Bridget received suitable remuneration. It seems incredible that anyone could peacefully continue ironing in the back room of a small house, no matter how sound its construction, with no awareness that two brutal murders were being done 50 feet away. Lizzie never accused Bridget, even in her hour of dire need, nor did her lawyers, perhaps at her request. Certainly Bridget returned to her native Ireland and lived in comfort until she returned to America — but to Butte, Montana, far from Fall River. There she married and lived on until 1948, 56 years after that scorching August morning. Where did she suddenly get the money?

Virginia Lincoln, however, adds a speculation that what really possessed Lizzie was temporal lobe epilepsy, a disorder associated with episodes of bizarre behavior. Now I view this suggestion with distaste. The diagnosis is not easy with the patient at hand and with all ancillary studies available. How, then, is one to take a little fact and a lot of fiction and come up with it 75 years after the event? Dr. Frederic Gibbs, my colleague and a noted expert in epilepsy, has studied the book and finds the evidence most tenuous.

Whatever possessed Lizzie, she is no longer a murderess, classic or otherwise. She has become an American legend, as Clytemnestra was in Greece. Her exploits have been the subject of novels, at least one play, a successful ballet aptly called "Fall River Legend," and an opera, successful as mid-twentieth century operas go. Some of the so-called true accounts contain as much fiction as fact, or more.

Then, too, Lizzie inspired the most familiar bit of doggerel in Americana and reams of verse less well known. Let us close our exploration of delight in evil by some stanzas of A.L. Bixby, entitled "To Lizzie":

> *There's no evidence of guilt,*
> *Lizzie Borden,*
> *That should make your spirit wilt,*
> *Lizzie Borden;*
> *Many do not think that you*
> *Chopped your father's head in two,*
> *It's so hard a thing to do,*
> *Lizzie Borden.*
>
> *You have borne up under all,*
> *Lizzie Borden,*
> *With a mighty show of gall,*
> *Lizzie Borden;*
> *But because your nerve is stout*
> *Does not prove beyond a doubt*
> *That you knocked the old folks out,*
> *Lizzie Borden.*

BIBLIOGRAPHY

De Quincy, T. *The English Mail-Coach and Other Essays,* Everyman's Library, No. 609. London: J. M. Dent, Ltd., 1961.

Gross, G. *Masterpieces of Murder,* An Edmund Pearson Crime Reader. Boston: Little Brown and Co., 1963.

Hodge, J.H. (Ed.) *Famous Trials 6: John George Haigh, 1949,* by Lord Dunboyne. Baltimore, Maryland: Penguin Books, Ltd., 1962.

Lincoln, V. *A Private Disgrace. Lizze Borden by Daylight.* New York: G. P. Putnam's Sons, 1967.

Pearson, E. *Murders that Baffled the Experts.* New York: Signet Books, 1967.

Radin, E.D. *Lizzie Borden: The Untold Story.* New York: Simon and Schuster, 1961.

Roughead, W. *The Art of Murder.* New York: Sheridan House, 1943.

Roughead, W. *Classic Crimes 1.* London: Panther Books Ltd., 1966.

Roughead, W. *Classic Crimes 2.* London: Panther Books Ltd., 1966.

Roughead, W. *Murder and More Murder.* New York: Sheridan House, 1939.

CHAPTER SIX

Et in Arcadia Ego

⌐

IN THE YEARS 1845 TO 1850, the Western World was torn by cata-
clysmic events which have influenced all subsequent history. There
were wars among the small German states and the Schleswig-
Holstein question began. A religious war raged in Switzerland.
From their refuge in Brussels, Engels and Marx published the *Com-
munist Manifesto.* The French and Austro-Hungarian territories in
what is now Italy were in revolt, as was Hungary. In France, the Revolution of 1848 toppled Louis Phillipe from the throne. This event
led to fear of French invasion of England just when the Chartist
Movement had revealed its full strength. There was a potato famine
in Ireland and mass emigration began. In Washington, threats of se-
cession were becoming ominous. In California, the chance observation of a strange radiance from certain pebbles in the tailrace of
Sutter's sawmill resulted in an increase of population from 15,000 to
250,000 in four years.

But there was one enclave of peace: Boston and its satellites,
Cambridge and Concord. The population of Boston itself was
130,000: 100,000 natives, principally of English descent, and 30,000
newly arrived immigrants from Ireland. The poor, confused Irish

---

Read at the Chicago Literary Club on November 22, 1971.

had as yet made little impression except to provide another outlet for the personal sort of charity which was then the obligation of gentle-folk. But the distinction of Boston's literary figures and educational institutions received international attention and the atmosphere was serene, if provincial. In 1842 Charles Dickens wrote:

> The air was so clear, the houses were so bright and gay, the signboards were painted in such gaudy colours, the gilded letters were so very golden, the bricks were so very red, the stone was so very white, the blinds and area railings were so very green, the knobs and plates upon the street doors so marvellously bright and twinkling, and all so slight and unsubstantial in appearance, that every thoroughfare in the city looked exactly like a scene in a pantomime.

The special character of Boston derived from its domination by an upper class of an unusual sort. The leading figures among the original settlers of Massachusetts had been people of good education and even more devotion to the cultural pursuits which education made possible. Their descendants prospered and intermarried. The control of the city was thus in the hands of a relatively small and hereditary group whose members combined integrity with intellectual attainments. They also had wealth, not great fortunes in the New York sense, to be sure, but substantial capital. The evolution of this class began with the early settlements of the Commonwealth, and in the 1840s it had been in full flower for some time.

To belong to it, money alone was not enough, intellect alone was not enough; both were essential. With them went a certain smugness. As a perceptive teacher of mine once remarked, "The Boston Brahmins had evolved the best system of living since the Greeks. The only trouble was, they knew it." When and how the upper class of Boston acquired the name *Brahmin* is not known for certain. One possibility is that it comes from the title of Emerson's poem "Brahma," published in *The Atlantic Monthly* in 1857. The class long antedated the poem, but the outcry which followed its appearance focussed attention on the name. Here are two of the stanzas, with their overtones of Transcendentalism and Oriental philosophy:

> *If the red slayer think he slays,*
> *Or if the slain think he is slain,*
> *They know not well the subtle ways*
> *I keep, and pass, and turn again.*

> *Far or forgot to me is near;*
> *Shadow and sunlight are the same;*
> *The vanished gods to me appear;*
> *And one to me are shame and fame.*

"To the average Western mind it is the nearest approach to a Torricellian vacuum of intelligibility that language can pump out of itself," pontificated Oliver Wendell Holmes. Emerson maintained an Olympian calm, his recorded remark being, "If you tell them to say Jehovah instead of Brahma they will not feel any perplexity."

Well might Oliver Wendell Holmes pontificate, for he was the arch-Brahmin of them all. Hardly five feet tall, he had the aggressiveness that often goes with small stature. His reputation as writer, wit, and pundit was considerable in the 1840s and his position as physician was secure. Among other medical publications, his paper, "The Contageousness of Puerperal Fever," which appeared in 1843, had already saved the lives of hundreds of women in childbirth. He was Dean of the Harvard Medical School as well as Parkman Professor of Anatomy and Physiology.

In fact, Harvard Medical School and the closely affiliated Massachusetts General Hospital were in a very productive period, in contrast to Harvard University across the Charles River in Cambridge, which was slumbering along under the not very energetic leadership of Presidents Edward Everett and Jared Sparks. The first public demonstration of ether as an anaesthetic in a major surgical operation was made by Dr. William T.G. Morton at the Massachusetts General Hospital in 1846, a landmark in medical history, though Dr. Charles Jackson disputed his priority. Dr. Holmes punned that the credit could go to ether.

Harvard Medical School also had a handsome new building in 1846, erected on land adjoining its affiliated hospital given by Dr. George Parkman. Dr. Holmes's professorship had been named in recognition of this gift. Dr. Parkman was a leading figure in financial and social Boston, but rather different from most of his fellow Brahmins. His tall, spare figure was a familiar sight as he rushed through the streets attending to his large real estate holdings, by means of which he had enlarged a substantial inheritance from his father into a large fortune. He wore a stovepipe hat, his coattails waved behind, and, in front, his lower jaw protruded so remarkably that he was called "Chin" behind his back. A medical graduate of Aberdeen, he had received further training under Dr. Philippe Pinel in Paris. He failed to secure the superintendency of the new McLean Hospital, a disappointment in the midst of successes. The only medical practice Dr. Parkman did was occasionally to attend the poor. However, he sometimes supported the scientific studies of others if he thought they were important. Audubon was so grateful for his help that he named a newly discovered species "Parkman's wren." A contemporary source characterized him thus: "The poor ever found in him a judicious friend — not indiscriminately lavish, nor blindly credulous. . . . The same rule governed him in settling an account involving a balance of a cent, as in transactions involving thousands of dollars. It was not the amount, but the precedent, that influenced him."

If Oliver Wendell Holmes was an example of the Brahmin physician with literary interests and Dr. Parkman the Brahmin financier-philanthropist, then Dr. John White Webster might represent the academician who lacked the other Brahmin qualification, money. He received a Harvard education and medical training at Guy's Hospital Medical School in London, where his signature on the register book appeared just above that of John Keats. In his maturity, Webster was a big, burly man with a massive forehead. His genial personality compensated for an unprepossessing appearance. He wrote and translated volumes on chemistry, served as editor of medical publications, and held membership in the American Academy of Arts and Sciences, the London Geological Society, and the St. Petersburg Mineralogical Society. The Ewing Professorship of Chemistry and Mineralogy was awarded to him in 1827, only 15 years after receiving his M.D. On the other hand, he was not an interesting teacher and his classroom experiments often failed.

This same sort of fecklessness marked his financial arrangements. A large inheritance from his father was used to build a splendid house on Harvard Street in Cambridge which he could not possibly maintain on a professor's salary. He had to sell it and move to a smaller one on Garden Street, but he still continued to entertain on a scale so lavish as to cause comment in order to keep up with such friends as Longfellow, whose wife, Fanny Appleton, was not only rich but beautiful. There were such distinguished visitors as Charles Dickens in 1842, who characterized Webster as having "personality and charm as well as considerable intellectual gifts." It was in that year that Webster began borrowing money from his friends, Dr. Parkman chiefly, but whoever would tide him over at the moment. In the next seven years, the borrowing spiraled, but Webster had the ability to overlook unpleasantness to a remarkable degree. Surface serenity covered a deep well of insecurity.

In the seventeenth and eighteenth centuries, many paintings bore the title, *Et in Arcadia Ego.* Each showed an idealized landscape with beautiful youths and maidens, but somewhere in shadow was a skull, a Death's Head, as a reminder that death was even in Arcadia. So, too, in the Arcadia of Brahmin Boston, death — violent death — lurked on November 23rd, the Friday before Thanksgiving in 1849.

On that day, Dr. Parkman did not return home for dinner at 2:30, the usual hour in the household as in most Boston homes at that time. What made this so remarkable was Dr. Parkman's obsession with time. If he were to be delayed, he invariably sent a message, and even this was seldom required. As afternoon passed into evening and evening into night without any word, consternation reigned at his home at 8 Walnut Street. By 8 o'clock next morning, Dr. Parkman's manservant was sent to the home of Robert Gould Shaw, Dr. Parkman's brother-in-law.

The manservant had admitted a caller whom he did not recognize between 8 and 9 A.M. on the day before and had heard him make an appointment with Dr. Parkman for half past one. Dr. Parkman had then called on Mr. Shaw and left at ten. A little after one o'clock he went to a grocery store near the medical school and asked that some sugar and butter be delivered to his home. He said he would shortly be back for a head of lettuce, at that time an expensive luxury in November, which he wished to take himself to his invalid daughter. Between half past one and two, two schoolboys saw Dr. Parkman walking toward the Medical School. From that point his where-abouts were unknown.

On Saturday evening, an advertisement in very small print ap-peared in the Boston newspapers asking for information about Dr. Parkman. This produced a sensation among Brahmins and com-mon folk alike. It was unheard of that a leading citizen of Boston should disappear, no matter what happened in the rest of the world. Shaw, who acted for the family, later inserted other advertisements offering first $3,000 for the discovery of Dr. Parkman alive, and then $1,000 for the finding of his body. Twenty-eight thousand handbills were distributed; the entire police force was mobilized; houses in the West End were searched; the Charles River was dredged. And all to no avail.

The time of year was especially conducive to the spread of ex-citement, for the coming Thursday was Thanksgiving. Families were assembling for this chief holiday of the New England year, mingling as it did religious observance, feasting, and family solidarity. As housewives brought the mincemeat from the buttery and laced it with what the abstemious called their "special flavorings," they spread the speculations about Dr. Parkman and remarked how sad it was for the family at this happy season.

On Sunday, the day after the advertisement appeared, Dr. Web-ster called on Samuel Parkman, Dr. Parkman's brother, and identi-fied himself as the man whom the manservant had let in on the day of the disappearance and stated that he and Dr. Parkman had met at 1:30, as planned. He had paid part of his debt to Dr. Parkman, Dr. Parkman agreeing to cancel the mortgage on his mineral collection. There was some cause for Webster's concern, for it was well known that he had borrowed heavily from Dr. Parkman, who held a mort-gage on his household effects and his mineral collection. By 1849 the debt amounted to $2,432, a large amount for Webster, since his total income from salary and student fees was about $1,900 per year. Dr. Parkman had made what might be called a public spectacle of his extreme indignation that Webster had sold his mortgaged cabinet of minerals to Robert Gould Shaw, his brother-in-law. With Parkman's conviction that charity is charity and business is business, he had demanded that the matter be set right at once or dismissal from the Medical School would follow. A disappearance could hardly be more opportune than Parkman's was for Webster.

Meanwhile, the newspapers of the whole country were filled with the story, and reports came in that Dr. Parkman had been seen in half a dozen cities — all of which proved unfounded. Gradually attention focussed on Harvard Medical School, since Dr. Parkman had not certainly been seen alive after his appointment there. On Monday two police officers made a casual search. The building, set as it was on the tidal shore of the Charles, was flush with the street at the front, but in the rear it rested on pilings. This allowed for a partial basement floor, which contained Professor Webster's laboratory and an apartment occupied by Littlefield, the janitor, and his wife. The search included the basement accommodation and was made in the presence of Dr. Webster and Littlefield. The police looked in the place where the waste from the dissection room was kept but had difficulty in inspecting the privy. It was after this search that Webster made Littlefield a gift of a Thanksgiving turkey, much in the spirit of the season but remarkable in that it was the first gift in the seven years of Littlefield's employment.

The gift, the repeated questions about the medical school, and the reward induced Littlefield to institute his own search, including the vault of the privy, which could only be reached by crawling under the pilings supporting the rear of the Medical School. With borrowed tools, he broke through only the outer layers of brick on Thanksgiving, though fortified by Dr. Webster's turkey. That evening he went to the Sons of Temperance Thanksgiving party and danced 18 of the 20 dances.

On the next day, Littlefield broke through the remaining layers of brick and what he saw sent him to his wife. As she later testified, "He bursted out a-crying," for there were objects looking suspiciously like human remains in the vault.

The police at once began a thorough search. They found portions of human remains in a chest containing tanbark and in the privy vault, and in the furnace there were charred false teeth, bits of bone, and a shirt button. Webster was immediately arrested at his home and brought to the city prison without a chance to speak to his family. So great was the excitement around the medical school that classes were suspended for three days and 5,000 curiosity seekers were admitted to the building.

The search for Dr. Webster's defense counsel ran into trouble. The first man approached was Daniel Webster. This was a failure which resulted in a hilarious confusion between Webster, the accused, and Webster, the advocate, when reported in the London newspapers. Then Rufus Choate was asked, but he would take the case only if Dr. Webster pleaded guilty. This was unthinkable to the accused and his friends. Other lawyers also declined to serve, and finally the court had to appoint counsel: Judge Merrick and Edward Sohier.

During the first two weeks of December, the jury of inquest was busy visiting the medical school, hearing testimony, and considering their verdict. On December 13th they reported that the remains were those of Dr. Parkman and that he had died at the Medical College from injuries by an unknown weapon which had been used by John W. Webster.

The trial began on March 19, 1850, with the Chief Justice of the Supreme Judicial Court of Massachusetts, Lemuel Shaw, presiding. Serving with him were three other judges ranging in age from 57 to nearly 80. The prosecutor was the politically ambitious Attorney General Clifford, whose junior counsel was George Bemis. Public excitement reached its climax with the opening of the trial. Newspapers from the entire Eastern seaboard, as well as those of London and Europe, covered the case in detail. The public was admitted, but in groups that changed every 10 minutes. In this way 55,000 to 60,000 caught a glimpse of the proceedings.

The task facing Attorney General Clifford was to prove that the remains found in Professor Webster's laboratory were not from a dissecting room subject; that they were all parts of one human body; that the body was that of Dr. Parkman; and that Professor Webster had done the murder and dismemberment. It was conceded that the body was not a dissecting room subject, for there was no trace of the chemicals used to preserve such material and the records showed no anatomical specimen missing.

A panel of Harvard physicians, headed by the anatomist Jeffries Wyman, testified that the remains found were all parts of one body, that of a man 50 to 60 years old (Dr. Parkman was nearly 60) and of the same height and build as Dr. Parkman. There was a good deal of body hair on the human fragments. A period touch was Mr. Shaw's embarrassment to have to state that he had seen portions of his brother-in-law's body unclothed and that they were remarkably hirsute. But confusion reigned as to whether the dismemberment had been done by an expert or by someone with little anatomical experience, or none at all. Oliver Wendell Holmes contributed to this dispute as an anatomist, but he also gave testimony for the defense that he heard no sounds from Webster's laboratory during his lecture in the room above at the crucial time.

The most important evidence for the identity of the body was given by Dr. Nathan Keep, a leading Boston dentist. In 1846 he had made a new set of false teeth for Dr. Parkman to wear at the dedication of the medical school built on the land he had given. Dr. Keep had kept the moulds and now produced them in court. Dr. Parkman's strange lower jaw, which had led to his nickname of "Chin," had required a most unusual form of block. After he had been fitted, he complained that there was no room for his tongue, and the blocks had to be specially filled. Those taken from the furnace bore the marks of the filling, and but for that, corresponded exactly with the moulds. Dr. Keep said that the false teeth must have been in the head when placed in the furnace, because otherwise they would have exploded in coming into contact with the fierce heat. He was a friend of both men and gave his evidence, which he knew to be crucial, under great tension. When halfway through, word came to Attorney General Clifford that the hotel at which he was staying was on fire. Court adjourned for 20 minutes while he removed his belongings. This waiting period completely unnerved the already tense Dr. Keep and he wept as he fitted the fragments from the furnace into the moulds.

Further evidence depended on handwriting. Soon after the disappearance, an illiterate letter was received by the police stating that Dr. Parkman had been taken on board the ship Herculan and another said that he had been murdered at Brooklyn Heights. Two more were signed "Civis," making suggestions for search. One of these was written at the end of November, but the other was received by Webster's attorneys while Webster was in prison. Curiously, only the first "Civis" letter was introduced in evidence. Penmanship experts differed as to how many had been written by Webster, but agreed that the first "Civis" letter matched his handwriting.

More important was the matter of the endorsement on Webster's notes. He wrote from jail that his wife should not open "the little bundle I gave her the other day." This set off another search of his home, which yielded a note for $400 plus another for $2,432 and memoranda in Webster's handwriting as to interest, including that on a note for $483.64 which he said he had paid. The interest calculated covered a period up to a date in 1850, a mistake Dr. Parkman would not have made. The larger note did not mature until 1851 and Dr. Parkman had not suggested that it be taken up. Both notes had signatures struck through. Even on Webster's story, he should not have had possession of the larger note.

The key witness that Webster had done the murder was the janitor, Littlefield, and his testimony was supported only by his wife. He was on the stand one whole day and until 2 o'clock the next. His statement was that he had overheard Parkman say at the 1:30 meeting on the day of the disappearance, "Dr. Webster, are you ready to-night?" and the reply, "No, I am not ready to-night, Doctor." Littlefield said he could not get into Webster's laboratory to do his work after that. He heard water running continuously hour after hour, though Prof. Webster disliked the sound of running water. The walls of the laboratory were hot, but there was little fire in the furnace. He then said he was tired of hearing that Dr. Parkman would be found at the medical school and instituted his own search, which led to the discovery. Prolonged cross-examination failed to shake him except on which day he received the gift of the turkey.

The defense relied on character witnesses, including Jared

Sparks, President of Harvard, on accounts of Webster's activities by his daughters, and on testimony of a few people that Dr. Parkman had been seen in Boston late on the afternoon of his disappearance. Dr. W. T.G. Morton, fresh from his quarrels over priority for the discovery of ether anaesthesia, gave dental testimony. He had not been supported by Dr. Keep in his contentions and now had a chance to confute him. Morton said that Dr. Parkman's jaw deformity was quite common and that he could fit the tooth fragments into many moulds, some of which he demonstrated.

Judge Merrick's speech for the defense left much to be desired. The jury was asked at one time to believe that Dr. Parkman was alive; at another that the remains were not his; that the remains were his but brought to the Medical School after death by an unknown murderer; that the evidence proved the guilt of Littlefield as much as Dr. Webster; that Webster killed Parkman but in circumstances to make it manslaughter.

Attorney General Clifford made a strong speech for the prosecution. At that time, a defendant could not give testimony in his own behalf but he could speak from the dock. This Webster did, berating his attorneys for not using the material he had prepared for them and calling dramatically for "Civis" to identify himself. No one responded.

Although it was already 5 o'clock, Chief Justice Shaw began his charge to the jury after a brief recess. This charge, now famous in legal history, will receive later comment. After three hours' deliberation, the jury returned a verdict of guilty. Sentence of death by hanging was given next day. The trial had lasted eleven days and sentence was pronounced on the twelfth.

This verdict increased the public uproar, if that was possible. Petitions were circulated in Webster's behalf and Parkman's character was roundly censured. The whole trial proceedings were bitterly condemned. An appeal to the Supreme Court of Massachusetts one month after the trail failed, as well it might, since its judges were the same as those at the trial.

Meanwhile, Webster was cheerful and maintained his habit of overlooking the unpleasant. He saw friends and enjoyed the food sent in from a nearby restaurant, for he was something of a gourmet. His family was his greatest concern and their daily calls his greatest comfort. But increasingly his mind turned to religion. The Reverend George Putnam called on him regularly and transmitted a confession from Dr. Webster to the Committee on Pardons. In it, Webster stated that he had killed Dr. Parkman in a sudden fit of rage and tried to dispose of his body when he saw ruin facing him. This failed to sway the Committee or Governor Briggs.

Execution was set for August 30th and was carried out in the yard of the Leverett Street jail. About 150 people assembled there, but all windows overlooking the jail yard were crowded. Webster bore himself with great dignity on the scaffold. That night his body was secretly removed by his lawyer, Sohier, and buried in an unmarked grave in Copp's Hill Burying Ground for fear of body-snatchers. In contrast, the remains in the medical school had long since been given a fine funeral, as befitted a leading Boston Brahmin.

So ended the grim business, and the crowds dispersed. Some of them took up the active Boston opera season, with performances of works by such recent composers as Rossini and Bellini. The *Transcript's* critic set each against his ideal, Mozart's *Don Giovanni*.

It is easy to overlook the fascination that murder had for all classes of Victorian society in Britain as well as the United States. Crowds at executions in England commonly reached 100,000 and sometimes 200,000. The 500,000 reported at one of them is probably exaggerated. Perhaps today the same impulses are served second-hand by the news media and are sobered by the violence of the professional killer. Then, too, there is the outlet of detective fiction. This had its beginning with Poe, who died in the year of the Parkman-Webster case. The Victorian age, perhaps because of this interest, produced a disproportionate number of those intricately plotted murders in real life which have been told again and again. Among the Victorians who had an exceptional interest in murder were Thackery and Dickens. One day, the two went together to a public execution, an experience which completely cured both of that form of entertainment. It also reduced their enthusiasm for capital punishment almost to the vanishing point. But Dickens wrote one formal detective novel and a few of his others approach that category. It is small wonder that the Parkman-Webster case held his attention, for he had met the executed man and knew many of those concerned. When he paid another visit to Boston in 1869, twenty years after the event, he promptly went to Harvard Medical School so that he might see the actual rooms where it took place. A letter to Lord Lytton recorded his impressions:

> Being in Cambridge, I thought I would go over to the Medical School, and see the exact localities where Professor Webster did that amazing murder and worked so hard to rid himself of the body of the murdered man. . . . They were horribly grim, private, cold, and quiet; the identical furnace smelling fearfully (some anatomical broth in it, I suppose), as if the body were still there; jars of pieces of sour mortality standing about, like the forty robbers in *Ali Baba* after being scalded to death; and bodies near us ready to be carried into next morning's lectures.

Edmund Pearson is justified in calling the case "America's Classic Murder." It fulfills with remarkable completeness the criteria for a murder that is to be told and retold. The lapse of nearly a century and a quarter has given to the ghastly events a period charm and a remoteness from the emotion-charged atmosphere of a recent crime. It gained significance because both Parkman and Webster were men of intellect, social standing and otherwise crimeless lives, despite their quirks. As De Quincy wrote, "Something more goes into the composition of a fine murder than two blockheads to kill and be killed — a knife — a purse — and a dark lane." The two people involved were not total strangers, but associates and close friends. "Only great criminals rise to the heights of a cooly planned murder of a friend or relative for gain," says Edmund Pearson. And the requirement of some fantastic detail to give a moment of relief from tension was provided by Littlefield's Thanksgiving turkey, Webster's first gift in seven years.

Most of all, the case has the attachment which comes from questions and dissatisfactions about the conduct of the trial and the verdict. The passage of more than a century leaves these issues as vital as they were at the time. There are large collections of source material on the case in several Massachusetts libraries, and they get good use. While I was working at the Boston Athenaeum, one of the librarians remarked, "There seems to be a procession — first Judge Sullivan, then a lady from Northwestern University, and now *you*." The books of my two predecessors are now in print. They are written from entirely different points of view.

The "Lady from Northwestern University," Mrs. Helen Thomson, has called her book "Murder at Harvard." It focusses on social history as related to the case. Based on a thorough study of primary sources and an extensive survey of historical writing, it brings together many details not otherwise known or not considered in this context. Her conclusion is that the trial was not fair but that Dr. Webster's confession is entirely true. The book, however, fails to make the substantial contribution which its scholarly background would lead one to expect for two reasons. The first is that the larger social issues involved are lost in masses of details, interesting though they are in themselves. The second is that Mrs. Thomson strangely chose to present the material by the technique of the "Had-I-but-known" school of detective novelists, complete with imaginary thoughts and conversations.

Judge Sullivan, on the other hand, has concentrated on the legal aspects of the case and has produced a document of permanent value. His study of all legal material bearing even remotely on his chosen interest has been thorough, but he makes little attempt to study the implications of the case beyond the law. The book is called, significantly, *The Disappearance of Dr. Parkman.* Its thesis is that Dr. Parkman simply wandered off or met with foul play at some undiscovered spot; that the body in Dr. Webster's laboratory was one dismembered by Littlefield to get the reward; that Dr. Webster never murdered anybody; that his defense was inept to an almost incredible degree; that the judge's charge to the jury was virtually a speech for the prosecution and had to be extensively revised before publication; that the appeal was improperly handled; and that Dr. Webster's confession was a hoax. All of these points have been suggested separately by Parkman-Webster students, but Judge Sullivan brought them together in an effective composite. The book is written from the standpoint of an astute defense attorney, whom Dr. Webster did not have, to his undoing. While Judge Sullivan does not fall into the trap of trying the case by current procedures, he points out the value of more recent changes in the law for the protection of the accused.

There is a background of distaste for Brahmin Boston and, in my own opinion, a limited understanding of it. These two factors result in some degree of bias, but it is the bias of the shrewd legal defender. The lay reader is fascinated by the skill with which Judge Sullivan treads lightly over difficult evidence, bears hard on the strong points, and introduces irrelevancies to divert attention from weaknesses.

At this point, it is only fair to ask my own opinion of the Parkman-Webster episode. As to the personality of Dr. Parkman, I do not fully agree with the lauditory contemporary accounts, but I also do not feel he was quite the ogre Judge Sullivan pictures. Trying, exacting, and brusque he surely was, but with an undercurrent of kindness, even if thanks were brushed off. There is no real evidence that Dr. Parkman's "aberration" was more than one of the "nervous breakdowns" fashionable in the nineteenth century. They were then often treated by rest and a sea voyage. The same malady now usually results in a visit to a psychoanalyst. As for Dr. Webster, charm and social distinction may or may not be matched by success in the class-room, hospital, or laboratory. He had periodic bouts of violent temper, as Mrs. Thompson points out. I do not agree with Judge Sullivan and others that Dr. Webster was not the type of man to murder. Murderers do not come to type. In the annals of classic crime, there are several undoubted murderers who were quiet, inoffensive men all their lives until they were driven to one great act of violence by a motive which at the moment was overwhelming. Consider, for instance, Dr. Crippen, whose name has passed into the English language as a minor oath. Pearson writes:

> To the public, he was a brutal and heartless wretch; but nobody who came in contact with him for one minute thought him

anything but a quiet, mild, courteous man. No act or word of unkindness to any living person could be produced against him. In court he was a marvel of composure; in prison he touched everyone by his unselfish devotion to the woman he loved.

I believe that the dismembered body was Dr. Parkman's. It piles coincidence upon coincidence to credit Littlefield with the production of a body of the correct age, physique, and hairiness on short notice. Judge Sullivan feels that the teeth were too much charred for critical study. He believes Dr. Morton's statement that the fragments would fit many sets of moulds. The moulds, which still exist at the Countway Library, show remarkable dental skill for the time and would be considered good work today. Fitting of any fragments into the moulds would add still more to the coincidences required by the anatomical evidence. The deformity of Dr. Parkman's jaw was unlikely to be as common as Dr. Morton testified, for the nickname "Chin" was reserved for Dr. Parkman alone. I have already given reasons why Dr. Morton may have been prejudiced in his testimony.

In a day and a half on the witness stand, Littlefield made only one minor error, about the day he received the gift of the turkey. Some lawyers feel that a witness who never varies his story is more suspect than one who makes a minor slip or two. If Littlefield made up his testimony completely and arranged for his wife to back it up, he would have had to have the plotting skill of Agatha Christie and Erle Stanley Gardner combined. No written record suggests that sort of brilliance.

The arithmetical error in calculating the interest on the note has received varying amounts of weight from different students of the case. To me, it is strong evidence that Dr. Parkman, so obsessive on matters of financial detail, did not make it. It is just the sort of mistake Dr. Webster was known to make again and again. If neither made it, how did it get on the note?

There can be no disagreement with Judge Sullivan that the defense was mishandled, as many felt at the time. In the 1920s the English barrister and judge, Lord Birkenhead, wrote an excellent analysis, stating that Judge Merrick's speech followed no clear line but suggested a number of defenses inconsistent with one another. He felt that procedure to be dangerous because a jury might take alternative arguments as evidence of a weak case. Judge Sullivan has carried the matter further by discovering the notes Webster prepared for his lawyers to use. These state that at the crucial times he was far away from Harvard Medical School, attending to his usual affairs. They contain many points which could have been checked and, if verified, made acquittal certain. I might suggest that some may have been checked and found erroneous. Several of Dr. Webster's other stories did not jibe with each other or with facts when investigated.

Judge Sullivan has done a real service in documenting the impropriety of Judge Shaw's charge to the jury and the extent of the revisions in the printed form. That the same judges should hear a case and then serve as the court to hear its appeal sounds more like Gilbert and Sullivan than legal procedure, but such was the Massachusetts judicial structure in 1850, and very little could be done about it *ad hoc.*

Like Mrs. Thomson, Lord Birkenhead, and many others, I believe Dr. Webster's final confession. Judge Sullivan writes, "Although there is no direct evidence, it seems likely that the Reverend Dr. Putnam could have volunteered to attempt to elicit a confession from Professor Webster, under the direction of the prosecution counsel and George F. Parkman, lawyer son of the deceased." He also points out that the Reverend Dr. Putnam, previously unknown to Webster, was closely acquainted with Attorney General Clifford, although Webster would not have known it. That this friendship would invalidate a confession transmitted by Putnam, I do not believe. Professor Webster was a deeply religious man with a vital belief in personal immortality. His final statement demands special consideration, even when transmitted by a minister who was a friend of the Attorney General. It seems natural that Webster should have turned to a stranger for the final consolations of religion instead of his own minister, who might be too closely connected with his family and with other aspects of the case.

If Professor Webster did indeed murder Dr. Parkman to protect himself and his family from financial disaster and disgrace, it is in some measure a crime which relates to the social environment in which it occurred. While this motive is strong in any society, the Brahmin combination of intellect, financial security, and smugness would give it a force not easy to match in another place and time.

One can only interpret the incomplete facts in the light of probability and one's own experience. To some extent, the same incompleteness of information gives all history its interest. As Lytton Strachy wrote: "Ignorance is the first requisite of the historian — ignorance, which simplifies and clarifies, which selects and omits, with a placid perfection unattainable by the highest art."

The end of the Parkman-Webster episode as a legal case brought no conclusion to its influence or interest. On the one hand, it set legal precedents still cited in the courts. On the other, those involved in the case and their descendants have figured significantly in subsequent American history.

It was in the Parkman-Webster trial that dental evidence was first accepted as proof of the identity of a body. It is now a legal commonplace, much refined in detail but still based on this precedent. It may have been easier to establish in Boston than elsewhere because it was remembered there that General Warren's body was identified in this way, though not in a court of law. At the Battle of Bunker Hill, the General's face had been so far destroyed as to be unrecognizable. Parts of the teeth containing silver wires were found and identified by the man who made them, no less a silversmith than Paul Revere.

As revised and published, Judge Shaw's charge to the jury has been cited for over 100 years in definition of such terms as reasonable doubt, circumstantial evidence, alibi, murder, and manslaughter by courts of the United States and Britain. Judge Sullivan's study leaves no doubt that the revisions were fundamental, but the final form has had a continuing influence when judges instruct juries in murder trials.

A less clear but highly probable result of the elaborate anatomical evidence and the doubts connected with it was the impetus it gave to the development of a professional medical examiner system in Massachusetts. This was established in 1877, the first in the United States.

It was clear even at the time that undue publicity had prejudiced a fair trial for Dr. Webster. We have made some progress in preventing repetitions of this, but not much. The Parkman-Webster case was cited as relevant in securing a closed hearing in the inquest on the incident at Chappaquiddick.

It is rather like Brahmin Boston that its ranks should soon close. Attorney General Clifford fulfilled his ambition to become Governor of Massachusetts. Varying fates were in store for those who gave evidence at the trial. Despite Littlefield's protests that he wanted nothing to do with the reward, he accepted a gift of $3,000, precisely the full amount offered, from Dr. Parkman's brother (by what euphemism is unknown) and thereupon disappears from recorded history.

Dr. Keep built up his reputation in Boston and became the first dean of Harvard Dental School. His opponent, Dr. Morton, pursued his controversy over the discovery of ether anaesthesia. There was sharp criticism when he attempted to patent his preparation under the name of "letheon." He died of a "neural disorder" in Central Park 18 years after the trial.

While Oliver Wendell Holmes was already the arch-Brahmin and Dean of Harvard Medical School, his career as a literary figure lay ahead. In 1853 he resigned as dean, but he retained an interest in medicine and, particularly, medical organizations, devoting more and more attention to writing. *The Autocrat of the Breakfast Table,* published in 1858, has become synonymous with his name. Several novels were only moderately successful at the time and are virtually unreadable today. However, some of them, especially *Elsie Venner,* are important in the history of the novel because they were among the first to incorporate psychology into this literary form. His light verse was widely admired and has provided its share of American clichés. At the time of the trial, his well-loved first-born son was a lad of nine. He was to carry the name of Oliver Wendell Holmes to international distinction as Associate Justice of the United States Supreme Court.

There is little more to tell of Dr. Parkman's brother-in-law, Robert Gould Shaw. This name is familiar now because of his grandson of the same name, who died leading his regiment of black troops in the Civil War. The incident has a fortuitous fame because the Robert Gould Shaw Memorial by Saint-Gaudens on Boston Common is one of the finest nineteenth-century American bronzes.

A meditation before it is William Vaughn Moody's best-known poem.

The end of the trial did not conclude the sufferings of the Webster and Parkman families. Mrs. Webster bore her troubles with dignity and courage but survived only three years after her husband's execution. Two daughters had already married and lived in Fayal; their two unmarried sisters sailed thence a few days after Mrs. Webster's death. One of them, Mrs. Dabney, returned to Cambridge, for Mr. Sibley, the retired Harvard librarian, recorded a visit to her in 1876. Miss Dabney, apparently the granddaughter, was a friend of Amy Lowell, the Brahmin poet. But the other members of the family remain lost in the mists of the Azores. Dr. Webster's professorship, its title now shortened to the Erving Professorship of Chemistry, has been held by a series of distinguished chemists. The present incumbent is Dr. Paul D. Bartlett, an internationally recognized authority on the physical chemistry of organic compounds. Into the laboratory where the events of 1849 occurred, there came in 1853 a young Brahmin chemist to study and teach. He never did develop into much of a chemist, but as President of Harvard University, Charles William Eliot became one of the most influential figures in American education.

The effect of the case on the Parkmans was at least as devastating as on the Websters. Mrs. Parkman and the invalid daughter became virtual recluses. The son never married but lived in a large house nearby. He left it as seldom as was compatible with the financial transactions by which he increased his substantial inheritance. When he died in 1908, he left his house and the residue of his estate for the maintenance of Boston Common and parks then existing. This amounted to $5,000,000. The house still stands unaltered externally, but it now has become the Institute of Contemporary Art.

The professorship named for Dr. Parkman remains on the books of Harvard Medical School but has not been awarded since 1941.

Dr. Parkman's nephew, Francis, had already made his trip along the Oregon Trail and published his now famous book on it in the same year as the murder. He became one of America's great historians, combining literary skill with scholarship. A commemorative stamp currently on sale is an indication of his enduring reputation.

Brahmin Boston as a social system survived the episode without a trace. There were, of course, the usual stories — sometimes true, often half true — but most were false. One of the better-authenticated examples concerned the cross-examination of a witness in court by the lawyer, Benjamin Butler. The questioning was so brusque that the judge reminded Butler that the witness was a Harvard professor. "Yes, I know, your Honor. We hanged one of them the other day."

As great numbers of immigrants arrived, especially from Ireland, the Brahmins came to make up a minute percentage of Boston population. With this change they seldom were influential in politics, but they retained control of financial and intellectual affairs out of all proportion to their numbers. It takes more than "America's Classic Murder" to put a crack in the monolith of Brahmin Boston.

> *"Far and forgot to me is near;. . . .*
> *And one to me are shame and fame."*

BIBLIOGRAPHIC NOTES

Unfortunately, no stenographic record was made at the Parkman-Webster trial. The most important published primary sources are: G. Bemis, "Report of the Case of John W. Webster" (Boston: Little and Brown, 1850) and *Member of the New York Bar,* "Trial of John W. Webster for the Murder of Dr. George Parkman" (New York: Cockcroft and Co., 1879). The newspapers of Boston, New York, Washington, London, Berlin, and other cities in 1849 and 1850 reported the case in detail. In this essay, chief use has been made of the *Boston Transcript* (*Boston Evening Transcript* 1849; *Boston Daily Evening Transcript* 1850). Of the many collections of manuscript material in Massachusetts libraries, that of the Countway Library of Harvard Medical School and the one in the Boston Athenaeum have been used for this paper. The two recent books referred to are: R. Sullivan, *The Disappearance of Dr. Parkman* (Boston: Little, Brown and Co., 1971) and H. Thomson, *Murder at Harvard* (Boston: Houghton Mifflin Co., 1971). A lively short account is E. Pearson, "America's Classic Murder, or the Disappearance of Doctor Parkman," in G. Gross (Ed.), *Masterpieces of Murder,* An Edmund Pearson True Crime Reader (Boston: Little, Brown and Co., n. d., pp. 53–67). An account of legal interest but flawed by a mistake in genealogy is "The Murder of Dr. Parkman" in Earl Birkenhead, *More Famous Trials* (London: Hutchinson and Co., n.d., pp. 183–192).

I thank Mrs. Franc D. Ingraham for arranging access to primary sources and many kindnesses, Samuel Parkman Shaw and Quincy Shaw for genealogical details, and Miss Catherine M. Fandell and Mrs. Richard Ford for helpful suggestions.

CHAPTER SEVEN

Migration and Nemesis

IN CHAPTER ONE I considered the changes in attitudes toward plants which result from migration in space and time. I also pointed out that equally great variations occur in the esteem of human beings when they move to another place or are viewed in the perspective of a different period. One of the characteristics of these changes in unpredictability. Neither botanical knowledge nor human psychology can forecast with assurance the effects which migration will produce.

Let us turn our attention to a physician who, a century ago, migrated from Chicago to London with results he did not forsee. It is without avail to think that he should have anticipated the consequences of his migration, for then, as now, the English look with less favor on murder than does the American judicial system. However, we view the matter in the perspective of a hundred years. Retrospection is notably fallacious in judging behavior, but it provides its moments of entertainment to students of human nature in unusual circumstances.

Our anti-hero, Thomas Neill Cream, was born on May 27, 1850, at 61 Wellington Lane, Glasgow. His father, William, was a man of good repute, perservering and prosperous. He emigrated with his

---

Read at the Chicago Literary Club on October 6, 1975.

wife and small children to Canada in 1854 or 1855: Neill (as he was usually known) was four or five years old when he first set foot on the North American continent. The father became manager of a thriving shipbuilding and lumber firm in Quebec. Having prospered, he apprenticed Neill to the shipbuilding trade, but already the young man's sights were on other things. At the age of 22 he entered McGill College for the study of medicine, and in 1876 he received his M.B. with merit. He was thought to have gained some distinction in his student days from an essay on chloroform. The medical school years were not without interest. He was well supplied with funds by his father which provided for flashy clothes, excessive jewelry, and a stylish carriage and pair. Such tastes could readily make a financial supplement desirable. At the beginning of his sophomore year, Neill insured his personal effects for $1,000. Curiously, there was a fire in his rooms 20 months later just before his graduation, the detailed claim for damages amounting to $978.40. Arson was strongly suspected, but the insurance company settled the claim for $350 and brought no criminal charges.

A few months before this, he was forced into a "shotgun" marriage to a girl on whom an abortion had been performed. The reluctant bridegroom left next day, ostensibly for England to pursue his medical training. Since nothing was proved in either case, he may readily have felt that such peccadilloes as abortion and arson would go unnoticed when perpetrated by Thomas Neill Cream.

At any rate, he was in London a few months after he received his M.B. and in October 1876 he became a post-graduate student at St. Thomas's Hospital. Although failing his examination for the Royal College of Surgeons in 1877, he passed those of the Royal Colleges of Physicians and of Surgeons in Edinburgh. With this double qualification he set off for Canada once more and opened a practice in London, Ontario. Not long after, the body of a chambermaid was found in a privy behind the premises occupied by Cream, a bottle of chloroform by her side. This incident recalls the student essay on that very chemical. It came to light that she had been frequenting his office to procure an abortion. The medical evidence ruled out suicide and indicated murder, the verdict being that she "died from chloroform, administered by some person unknown." The good folk of London, Ontario, took so dim a view of the situation that his practice was ruined.

The doctor next appeared in Chicago, where he did himself rather well by setting up practice at 434 West Madison Street (now 1255). In 1880 this was a neighborhood of substantial houses, green lawns, and fine trees. Horse-cars provided good public transportation for his patients and fair weather seemed ahead. However, he quickly acquired a reputation as an abortionist. When that on Julia Faulkner ended fatally, Cream was arrested, but the evidence was not conclusive and he went scot free. Four months later, another of his patients, Miss Stack, died after taking medicine prescribed by Cream, and the body was found in an outhouse behind his home. A month after the death he tried to blackmail the pharmacist who filled the prescription. This persecution was put to an end by a more serious problem for the doctor.

It so chanced that at that exact time our versatile physician was advertising a specific cure for epilepsy. The disease in 1881 was a good one for a profitable nostrum, since its cause and effective treatment were then unknown. The ensuing century has brought rational therapy and some clarification of cause, but both still are imperfect. In 1881 the disorder was as common as it is today, but few then suffering from it reached the neurologists practicing in Chicago, though there were several distinguished ones. Most epileptics relied on patent medicines, attracted more by flamboyant labels than by medical considerations.

Daniel Stott, a 61-year-old station agent on the Northwestern Railroad in Grand Prairie, Illinois, suffered from this disorder. Not being able to travel frequently to Chicago, he sent his pretty wife of 33 to get the famous remedy. In fact, she made the trip for fresh supplies at ever shorter intervals, as the attraction between the young woman and the 41-year-old benefactor of epileptics ripened into more than friendship. On June 11, 1881, yet another prescription was required, and it was filled at a nearby drugstore. Mrs. Stott asserted later that Dr. Cream added a white powder to it and also to some rhubarb pills which she got for her husband at the same time. Three days afterward, Mr. Stott took the medicine and died within twenty minutes. Meanwhile, Cream had been trying to insure his patient's life, but the policy was not yet in effect.

The death was readily attributed to an epileptic seizure, and all would have been well for him had matters been left to rest. However, Cream inexplicably informed the coroner of Boone County that the pharmacist had put too much strychnine in the medicine and demanded an exhumation. Receiving no cooperation from the coroner, the doctor next approached the district attorney, who took action. On analysis of the exhumed body, four grains of strychnine were demonstrated in the stomach.

At this point the doctor found his troubles compounded, since he was out on bail for a charge of sending scurrilous matter through the mails. His flight to Canada ended near Windsor, Ontario, where he was taken into custody. He and Mrs. Stott were indicted for murder on his return to Chicago. Mrs. Stott turned State's Evidence and, indeed, had probably been a passive onlooker. After due meditation by the jury, Dr. Cream was found guilty of murder, but in the second degree. On November 1, 1881, he began a life sentence at Illinois State Penitentiary at Joliet. At that point, McGill struck the name of Thomas Neill Cream from its roster — a casual way to treat one of its well-remembered graduates.

The official description at that time recorded him as of stout and solid build, with massive head and thinning hair. He was 5 feet 9 inches tall, and there was a squint to his light gray eyes. The years at Joliet passed quietly — perhaps too quietly for his taste. In 1890 he wrote to Pinkerton's National Detective Agency, asking it to trace Mrs. Stott in the hope that she would give an affidavit in his favor. She was never found.

Meanwhile, Cream's father had died in 1887, leaving him $16,000, a substantial capital in those days. Edmund Pearson describes the sequel somewhat brusquely:

> Sympathizers thought that the time had come to give the poor fellow another chance, with the opportunity to enjoy himself and his inheritance. An agitation was begun to effect his release; Mr. Stott was dead, and doubtless anybody who opposed the commutation would have been denounced as revengeful.

At any rate, on June 12, 1891, Governor John W. Fifer reduced the sentence to 17 years, with allowance of time for good conduct, bringing the term to its conclusion on July 31, 1891, after not quite ten years in the penitentiary. Perhaps the governor felt that to deny the doctor his patrimony was "cruel and unusual punishment," which is forbidden in the Eighth Amendment.

So the doors of Joliet swung open and Prisoner 4374 again became Dr. Thomas Neill Cream, L.R.C.P. and L.R.C.S. (Edin.) and in a strong financial position. He hastened to claim as much of his patrimony as his father's executors would let him have, ostensibly to visit England for his heath.

Chicago seemed to attract our anti-hero no longer, but he may not have paused long enough to sense the vigor and intellectual ferment that had come to it in his decade at Joliet. The city had quite suddenly developed into a world center of modern architecture, with Adler, Sullivan, and the young Frank Lloyd Wright designing such monumental buildings as the Auditorium, the Ryerson Building, and, in domestic architecture, the Charnley residence. It is true that not all the building was so forward-looking, for the Potter Palmer pseudogothic mansion struck a reactionary note, to say the least. But the owner had already begun to embellish its walls with French Impressionist paintings, eventually to become one of the most distinguished collections in private hands and to exert a significant force in the recognition of these artists.

Neither did he pause long enough to learn that the Chicago Literary Club, a lusty infant when he entered Joliet, was now grown to full stature as a social and intellectual institution or to realize the significance of the fact that Clinton Locke was preparing to give his Inaugural Address a month hence on "The Making, Giving and Receiving of Taffy."

There had been a few changes in the neighborhood of West Madison and Racine, and those were for the better, since cable cars had replaced the horsecars he remembered. In so substantial a neighborhood, Cream would have been justified in feeling that its good people might not readily entrust their medical problem to a newly released murderer. He could not know that the district in a few years would begin the *descensus Averno* which was to become so extreme. A recent visit showed that the desolation was absolute. No footsteps broke the silence of the sidewalks and no car passed along the street. The site of Cream's dwelling is now a vacant lot, with the low building of the American Offset Company hard by. The rest of the block is occupied by sleazy shops, most of them untenanted, and across the street there is the Stop and Eat Grill, an injunction which I did not heed.

In view of the activities that coming events showed Cream to have already in mind, he may not have considered the advantages offered to carry them out in Chicago. The police force was meager, with 1680 patrolmen to cover 181 square miles, or 1 to 715 inhabitants. The officers were mostly concerned with assault, arrests on this charge having increased 30 times while Cream smoldered at Joliet. Prostitutes were available in numbers, for a newspaper of the day stated that efforts had not eliminated "the polluting presence of abandoned women who wandered through the streets."

With advantages ranging from creative architecture to uncontrolled prostitution, how could the good doctor have looked elsewhere? But that is precisely what he did. He took passage on the *Teutonic* and arrived at Liverpool just two months after Joliet sent him forth. As befitted a man newly come into his inheritance, he chose this newest and finest ship of the White Star Line. It was so grand, in fact, that when the Prince of Wales was showing his nephew, Kaiser Wilhelm II, its splendors, Kaiser Bill remarked rather grandly, "We must have some of those." What elicited the Kaiser's envy should surely have been adequate for Dr. Cream. Among the amenities of the ship, there was a barber shop with an entrance resembling a cathedral vestry, and inside it, the hairbrushes were driven by electric motors. The woodwork everywhere was dark mahogany; stained glass and electric lamps abounded. Electricity was then a novelty and rare even in the stately homes of England.

The doctor traveled alone. Perhaps this was again due to a

desire for creature comforts unalloyed. Even though the *Teutonic* held the Atlantic Blue Riband for a passage of five days, 16 hours, 31 minutes, a lady would have had required corsets rigid with whalebone stays and petticoats in number and variety, to say nothing of the voluminous dresses — broadcloth for morning strolls on deck, grenadine for afternoon tea, velvet brocade for evening, and voided velvet for the captain's dinner.

No, he traveled without feminine companionship, or so he thought. But he was quite wrong. There was a woman with him all the way. She encroached on his living quarters not at all, for her luggage consisted only of a measuring rod, a bridle, a sword, and a scourge. She stayed by his side even unto the end, but his end, not hers. And she was invisible, for this was the goddess Nemesis, the bringer of divine retribution.

Unaware of his ghostly companion, Dr. Cream disembarked on October 1st at Liverpool and proceeded at a leisurely pace to London, not arriving until the fifth. This was wise, for a busy month lay ahead. The devil within him, long caged, had come out roaring. Consider the dates: October 1st, landed in Liverpool; October 5th, arrived in London; October 7th, moved into permanent lodgings; on or before the 12th, bought strychnine; 13th, first murder; 20th, second murder.

Now for a closer look at these activities. On arrival in London, he registered as Dr. Neill at Anderson's Hotel in Fleet Street. Next day, under the name of Dr. Thomas Neill he engaged a front room on the second floor of 103 Lambeth Palace Road, to which he moved the following morning. The street wanders along the South Bank of the Thames past Lambeth Palace, the home of the Archbishop of Canterbury. This great edifice was to be a mute onlooker to the strange scurryings of the doctor, as he rushed about in flowing coat and stovepipe hat, bent on devil's errands. Dr. Cream was not the first nor the last evildoer that the grim and holy pile had watched, for the streets around it were then seedy and depressing. The years have changed them somewhat by the development of new buildings for St. Thomas's Hospital in the 1960s, in the course of which Dr. Cream's lodgings were demolished. A physician in the full professional dress of the day could hardly have been an inconspicuous figure in such surroundings.

The evening between engagement of his new home and moving in was wet and dismal (as evenings often are in a London October). Solace came when he met a woman of the streets named Elizabeth Masters in Ludgate Circus near his hotel. The silent majesty of Wren's masterpiece watched unmoved as the girl and her companion drank wine at the King Lud pub and then went to Gatti's Music Hall. When they returned to the pub to round out the evening, they were joined by Elizabeth May, a friend of Masters. When it was time to say good night Cream promised another meeting. Three days later, an appointment having been made by letter, the two girls watched at their window, only to see the doctor come along the street with Matilda Clover, whom they knew slightly. She was a pleasant looking brown-eyed girl with prominent teeth. May and Masters followed and saw the couple enter Clover's home and they waited for him, but the doctor had not emerged after an hour.

Three days after this incident, the poison book of Mr. Priest, chemist, recorded the purchase of strychnine by "Dr. Thomas Neill, M.D." On the next day, a man in Waterloo Road noticed a girl leaning against the wall and then falling to the street. He went to her assistance, though such an event was common enough in that neighborhood as to occasion little notice. Her name was Ellen Donworth, another prostitute of the area. She was in great pain but was able to explain that a tall gentleman had given her "white stuff" from a bottle. Convulsions developed and she died on the way to the hospital, where a post-mortem proved poisoning by strychnine. This became known as the Lambeth Mystery, which was deepened when a letter signed "A. O'Brien, Detective" offered to name the murderer for the small fee of £300,000. Another letter from "H. Bayne" to W.H. Smith and Son named a member of the firm as the murderer but offered to save him if H. Bayne was retained as barrister. A paper was to be posted on the window as acceptance. Following police instructions, this was done, but H. Bayne remained elsewhere.

Exactly one week later, the screams of Matilda Clover, whom we have met before, broke the night quiet of Lambeth Road at 3 A.M. In pursuit of the oldest profession in the world, she again received that evening the tall man in flowing overcoat and tall hat. During a momentary respite in her agony, she said that she had been poisoned by pills give her by "that man." The death, however, was certified as due to alcoholism.

About a month later, Dr. William H. Broadbent of Portman Square received a letter from one "M. Malone," accusing him of murdering Matilda Clover with strychnine (which was the first time that poison had been mentioned). Dr. Broadbent was one of the most distinguished London physicians at the time and was later knighted. His name is still familiar to medical students, for Broadbent's sign remains important in the diagnosis of adhesive pericarditis. Again on police advice, a trap was laid, but M. Malone was reticent. In December, the Countess Russell, who was staying at the Savoy Hotel, received a letter accusing her husband, the Earl, of the murder.

With these exciting events accomplished, the devil within was satiated and for three months it rested. Then it sprang forth with redoubled ferocity. On April 11, a police constable saw Emma Shrivell let out of her lodgings at two A.M. a man in a tall hat, a street lamp giving the officer a good opportunity for observation. Within an hour, shrieks rent the night air not only from Shrivell but also her companion, Alice Marsh. Between convulsions, they told their land-lady that a tall man had given them capsules, which they dutifully swallowed. Marsh died on the way to the hospital, but Shrivell en-dured her sufferings for five hours more.

Scotland Yard now realized that it was dealing with a systematic murderer, operating by the use of strychnine on prostitutes specifi-cally in Lambeth. Exhumation of Matilda Clover's body was not easy, as fourteen coffins had to be moved to reach it. Autopsy showed that her death, too, was due to strychnine and not alco-holism.

It soon became known to the police that not all the intended victims were so docile as to take the medicine so generously pro-vided by the doctor. To Violet Beverly he offered an "American drink," but she was loyal to her British heritage and chose beer. Her patriotism was much to her advantage, for the drink almost surely contained a good quantity of the doctor's white powder. It also may be regarded as a tribute to her palate, considering what some Lon-don hotels and pubs still serve as an "American cocktail."

From January 7 to April 1, 1892, Cream was traveling in Canada, crossing the Atlantic less grandly than before. In Quebec he ordered the printing of 500 circulars for delivery in London, stating that Ellen Donworth's murderer was employed at the Metropole Hotel and the lives of its guests were in danger. These extraordinary leaf-lets were never used.

In May, one month after the double murder, Sergeant McIntyre of Scotland Yard met by accident one Dr. Neill. The doctor said he was being followed and harassed by the policemen who accused him of murdering Marsh and Shrivell. This was news to the police. He also said that he had a letter written before their deaths stating that they should beware of a Dr. Harper, lest he serve them as he had Clover and Lou Harvey. This was the first that had been heard of Lou Harvey. Efforts to find her body were unavailing, for the good and sufficient reason that she turned up alive, healthy and able to give the police some interesting information. On her second meeting with the tall, silk-hatted man, he offered her some pills for her complexion, but she was astute enough to drop them surreptitiously on the ground.

Early in June, Dr. Neill was arrested for blackmail, which charge was altered to murder a month later. The trial at the Old Bailey in October was for the murder of Clover. It touched upon legal problems of the time at only one point: This was whether evidence of the other crimes could be admitted to show system and method. The judge ruled that it could, at which point conviction was a certainty. Girls who had seen him with Clover, the constable outside Shrivell's house, and Lou Harvey all identified the doctor. He was found in possession of strychnine. It took the jury only ten minutes to find him guilty, and on November 15, 1892, Nemesis exacted her final retribution in the yard of Newgate Prison.

This strange tale has attracted many writers, good, bad, and indifferent. Shore's account is the most detailed, but Pearson's is the most entertaining by virtue of what I have called his "delight in evil." De Quincy, over a century ago, laid down the criteria for including a murder in the select group of vintage crimes in his essay, "On Murder Considered as One of the Fine Arts." Let us see how far Dr. Cream meets the requirements.

One is that the murderer should previously have led a blameless life. In this respect, the doctor notably fails to qualify. A career that included arson, wife desertion, sending improper material through the mail, criminal abortions with fatalities, and blackmail could hardly be said to have been blameless.

Another criterion is that there should be no gross violence. One thug beating another thug to death is for the newspapers and not the connoisseur of murder. Cream meets this requirement: a little white powder, a short period of agony while the murderer is far away, and the deed is done. There is some disagreement among the experts on the inclusion of poisoners in the select group of murderers. De Quincy decries them, but Pearson comments, "Of all sly deviltry, the art of the poisoner is unsurpassed." I agree with Pearson.

There is the requirement of all the authorities that the victim should be a relative or close friend, for such an act tries the crassest soul to its depths. Here Cream is marginal. All the London girls he had seen not more than two or three times before he favored them with his medicine, and in the Chicago exploit, it was the wife of the victim and not the victim himself who was his friend. Perhaps Cream made friends with unusual speed, and speeding is dangerous.

Then, too, the arbiters decree that there should be an element of mystery or terror. In this case, one element of mystery has been created by the biographers themselves; this regards Cream's nationality. The facts are plain enough: born in Scotland, reared in Canada, first tasted the heady wine of murder in Chicago, and in London drained the cup. British writers usually describe him as an American doctor. Pearson remarks:

> There is often a marked tendency, outside this country, to be hazy about the birthplace or political allegiance of such Americans as Sargent, Whistler, and Edwin Abbey — and this is natu-

ral. The English journalist, to do him justice, usually awards us Doctor Crippen, but he errs on the side of generosity when he also attributes Doctor Neill Cream to America.

A more genuine bit of suspense is afforded the sensitive observer as he considers whether each girl will take the medicine or discard it quietly. There would have been a strong element of mystery, or no story at all, if the doctor had not persisted in his idiotic elaboration. Of the murderer, Pearson writes:

> If he can keep his head, if he does not talk, and if he is remorseless, human society, it has been said, is at his mercy. There have been murderers so equipped, but they have usually tried to repeat their success too many times.

Cream was completely remorseless, but in keeping his head he was an utter failure. It is true that his activities were repetitious, but that alone is not sufficient. In fact, Pearson has pointed out that his Rule 4 for murderesses applies equally to men: "If you commit murder for insurance money, or for mere pleasure, make it wholesale. Never stop at one."

What impelled the man Dr. Cream is a moot question. It was surely not for insurance money. This appeared only in the Chicago episode, but the murder occurred before the policy was in effect. There is no evidence that he wished to legalize a relationship with Mrs. Stott. Was it for mere pleasure? Very possibly, if pleasure be construed as satisfaction in giving full rein to a trait of personality unacceptable to the laws and conventions of society.

Was the mental structure of this man so warped that he would be called insane? Insanity has legal definitions, but its medical limits are less easy to delineate. Cream was tried under the M'Naghten rulings. In simplified form, these state that a person is responsible for his crime if at the time it was committed he knew right from wrong and that what he was doing fell into the latter category. His elaborate attempts to protect himself after the event are sufficient evidence to show his own knowledge that he had committed crimes for which he might suffer penalty. Taken with the other evidence, there can be no doubt that the verdict of "guilty" was justified at the time of the trial.

But would it be today, nearly a century later? An astute defense attorney would point to the ineptitude of the coverup, the multiplicity of the murders, and lack of motive as evidence of insanity. The systematic poisoning of prostitutes, each with an identical poison, would now tell in his favor, instead of being his Nemesis, as in 1892. The same evidence, bolstered by expert psychiatric testimony, would almost surely result in a verdict of "Not Guilty by Reason of Insanity." Then would follow a period of incarceration in an institution for the criminally insane until his reason should be thought to have returned. Cream was a plausible fellow and made friends all too readily, as we have seen. It is quite likely that he could have quite quickly convinced his examiners that he had regained a full state of mental health. He would then be free to do it again until the number of his exploits could have equalled the conquests of Don Giovanni in Spain — "mille e tre."

The legal interest in this case lies in two points. We have already considered the admissibility of evidence from other crimes to show method, which is still decided individually in different cases and may be favorable to the prosecutor or the defense, depending on the circumstances.

The other long-range legal consideration is its relevance to capital punishment. Those who favor this penalty point out that at least four young people could have lived to know the joys and sorrows of many years if Governor Fife had taken an attitude more like that of the English judiciary system. To me, capital punishment is repugnant, but I also view with some alarm the speedy release of murderers judged insane when they receive an inheritance or are simply "nice fellows."

In another respect, this episode fulfills the requirements for a notable crime — that it should be remote in time and divorced from the emotions and pressures of the day in which we live. Almost a century has passed since the stirring deeds of Dr. Cream. It is an exercise in social history to recapture the atmosphere in which they took place. The ancient monuments that watched over these memorable events remain unchanged and unchanging, but the modes and pace of daily life have altered beyond recognition. In attempting to bring into focus this little segment of the past, I am encouraged by a statement of G.M. Trevelyan:

> To discover in detail what the life of man on earth was like, a hundred, a thousand, ten thousand years ago is just as great an achievement as to make ships sail under the sea or through the air. How wonderful a thing it is to look back into the past as it actually was, to get a glimpse through the curtain of old night into some brilliantly lighted scene of living men and women . . . warm-blooded realities even as we are.

If I were to choose one day from this story as most worth recall, I would select October 6, 1891, when the doctor rushed about the streets in quest of lodgings, until the rainy, dismal evening brought respite in wine, music hall, and feminine companionship. St. Paul's watched, serene and aloof, while the pagan goddess Nemesis guided his footsteps through the wet, dark streets with their fitful gleam of gaslight, as he strode inexorably onward to the culmination at New-gate.

But it is not the Ultimate that the insubstantial goddess of rod and bridle, scourge and sword should bring a final retribution. More often than not, Time will clear away the rubble of our daily round and expose to view the Wise, the Noble, and the Compassionate. That is the substance of our hope.

PART THREE

The Harvard Society of Fellows

Where shall wisdom be found and where is the place of understanding? Surely it should be . . . where men are most free to think and write their own thoughts.

ABBOTT LAWRENCE LOWELL,
WHAT A UNIVERSITY PRESIDENT HAS LEARNED

CHAPTER EIGHT

Ask the Concierge

⤳

ACADEMIC FREEDOM, like other terms used to symbolize abstractions, means different things to different people and to the same person at different times. It may be the freedom of an individual holding an academic appointment to express in public views not generally shared by his colleagues. Again, it may be the freedom to engage in political activity while on the staff of a university, perhaps in unconventional directions.

It is none of these forms of academic freedom which I wish to consider here. There is also that form of academic freedom which concerns the pursuit of study, investigation, and research in whatever way and to whatever end will lead to the fullest realization of an individual's ability. Here we are concerned with the sort of environment which best serves academic freedom in this sense, principally through a discussion of a notable experiment: the Society of Fellows of Harvard University.

Abbott Lawrence Lowell, distinguished historian and president of Harvard for twenty-five years, gave deep consideration to the problem of academic freedom in all its aspects throughout his long life. He said on many occasions, "I am often asked to define aca-

Read at the Chicago Literary Club on January 6, 1964.

demic freedom. I find it impossible to do so in a sentence, but I can illustrate it with an anecdote":

> There was once a young Frenchman in a provincial university who was awarded a professorship at the Collège de France. When he arrived in Paris, he went each day for a week to his classroom, and nothing happened. Bewildered, he sought out one of his senior colleagues and asked, "What are my duties as Professor here?"
>
> The old scholar replied, "Oh, your duties are to get on with your work, and if you have any questions — umm — ask the concierge."

"That," said Mr. Lowell, "is academic freedom."

Such an environment has, indeed, been the distinguishing characteristic and particular glory of universities since the twelfth century. In fact, the degree with which these conditions have been created is the most cogent measure of the excellence of a university.

There is far less unanimity on how this environment is to be entered and at what stage of training and development a young person can best be entrusted to the concierge as mentor. Two approaches have been made historically: the English system, with its tutorial system and rather vaguely defined curriculum; and the German, with formal prescribed course work and thesis, leading to the degree of Doctor of Philosophy. American universities, at their inception, derived from the English model but were transformed in the latter part of the nineteenth century into something like the German, owing in large part to the influence of Charles William Eliot after his selection as president of Harvard in 1869.

Doubts about this rigid sort of graduate education have appeared from time to time, and never more seriously than at Harvard in the decade following the end of World War I. It was in this setting that Alfred North Whitehead arrived there at the age of 64, only one year before he would have retired from his post at the University of London. He made the transition between the two countries as easily intellectually as he did physically and pursued a new and distinguished career from that time until his retirement at 75. He did, however, miss the occasions for formal conversation which were so much a part of his life in London and the English Cambridge.

In fact, he decided to create a place for it in the American Cambridge. He and Mrs. Whitehead, a more glittering and almost equally profound conversationalist, let it be known to a selected group of friends and colleagues that they would be at home every Sunday evening. These evenings were devoted to what is usually called Victorian conversation, though why this should be named after the great Queen I have never been able to fathom, unless its serious tone would have suited that grave Monarch. Certainly it had become a fine art in eighteenth-century England, with Dr. Johnson as its high priest. Certainly, also, it flourished in the salons of Paris at least as brilliantly as in the parlors of Windsor.

Now what is meant by Victorian conversation? It is an exchange of ideas on a selected topic from different points of view, not random talk ranging over anything which turns up. I cite a familiar example. In the last years of the nineteenth century, William James and Percival Lowell, the great astronomer and brother of Abbott Lawrence, each had a "nervous breakdown," as was fashionable at that time. Their physician sent both of them off to the Riviera to recuperate. When it was thought that they had improved sufficiently to meet, an evening of conversation was arranged. It was decided that James should select the topic and Percival Lowell give a definition. The subject proposed was "Virtue," which Lowell immediately defined: "Virtue is the belated compensation for the sins which one has neglected to commit." It is difficult to imagine what course the subsequent conversation could have taken.

Or, to choose an example from Mr. Whitehead on an occasion when I was present, the subject he selected was "Grass." He went on to say that all the differences between Englishmen and Americans could be explained by the contrasts in their attitude toward grass. In America, "Keep off the grass" signs were everywhere, but nobody paid much attention, whereas the Englishman was so bound by the tradition of the sacredness of grass that no signs were required. From there, we discussed national characteristics and in how far they actually exist.

It would give an incomplete picture of the Whiteheads' Sunday evenings if one failed to note the setting in which they took place. Wherever they lived (and they moved several times), there were large, book-lined rooms, as might be expected. The surprise was that the walls and woodwork were everywhere painted flat black. There were many large light pictures with wide white mats, chairs upholstered in ivory, and always drifts of white flowers, so that the black formed hardly more than an accent, but its strangeness and, at the same time, its beauty remained. I had thought this a personal and ingratiating eccentricity of Mrs. Whitehead until I recently came across a statement of Alice B. Toklas about Paris in the early years of this century: "In those early days she lived in a flat in the rue Bisson-ade, which was painted in the fashionable manner of the day in black." Now Mrs. Whitehead was brought up in Paris at just that time, and she apparently clung to a fashion of her girlhood through-out her long life.

On these evenings, the problems of the developing scholar found careful consideration. The Whiteheads were not alone in this concern, for at the time it was the custom of Professor Henry Osborne Taylor to invite a group to his home in Connecticut for discussions, a sort of intellectual house-party. On one of these occasions, Mr. Whitehead talked at length about the over-teaching of graduate students with Lawrence Joseph Henderson. Mr. Henderson, though best known for his application of physical chemistry to biological problems, was really a Renaissance man in the twentieth century. I note that at the time of his death, he was teaching a course in biological chemistry, another in the history of science, and two more in sociology. It was generally thought that he also could have given a better course in modern French literature than anyone in the Romance Language Department. A more worthy colleague for Whitehead would be hard to find.

As these two men talked about the checks on the originality of graduate students which resulted in the American university from close concentration on a definite examination, both were conscious of conditions in England, particularly at Cambridge, and also in Paris. Mr. Henderson felt that this sort of freedom for graduate students ought to make its appearance in the United States. Mr. Whitehead pointed out that the system of education, like so many things in England, had not been a sudden or logical development but had come about by chance. At Trinity College, Cambridge, there were fellowships for six years, during which time their holders might do any form of work they liked. They came in contact with other people in all sorts of fields at the dinner table in the college hall. Much of the advantage of these fellowships resulted from the association of people in different fields, not over-pressed with assigned work. There was no separation of the teacher and the taught; older and younger members met freely on equal terms.

As Whitehead and Henderson made the slow journey from New London to Boston by the New York, New Haven and Hartford, the conversation continued and an idea began to take concrete form. If any organization like that at Trinity could be established at Harvard, it would be possible to pick a group of men who would profit from the associations. Henderson proposed that they call on President Lowell the next day and put their idea before him.

When, as planned, Mr. Henderson began his explanation to Mr. Lowell, the latter went to a cupboard, unlocked it, pulled out some notes, and said, "I have been thinking of something like that for years and have been waiting to put it in effect." The idea which Mr. Lowell had formulated derived more from the Fondation Thiers in Paris than from Trinity College. He felt that there should be a small house in which young men, freed from the burden of routine responsibilities, might live together and exchange ideas. Mr. Lowell asked that his plan be compared with that of his visitors and that a committee be formed to draw up concrete proposals. John Livingston Lowes, the Chaucerian authority and author of *The Road to Xanadu,* and Charles Curtis, a Boston business man of scholarly attainments, joined Whitehead and Henderson in what came to be known as the Committee of Four.

The committee began its report by citing results: "One-half of the British Nobel prize winners, one-fifth of the civil members of the Order of Merit, and four of the five Foulerton Research Professors of the Royal Society have been Fellows of Trinity College, Cambridge. At present every officer of the Royal Society is a Trinity man. Other honors and distinctions in almost equal profusion have, during the past half century, fallen to the lot of the Fellows and former students of the College of Bacon and Newton, of Dryden, Byron and Tennyson, of Macaulay and Thackeray, of Clerk Maxwell and Rayleigh."

This was written in 1926. I do not know whether these proportions would hold in 1964, but I note that the current Foulerton Professor was a fellow of Trinity, as were both of the 1963 English Nobel Laureates in Physiology and Medicine.

The report favored an organization much more nearly that of Mr. Henderson than that of Mr. Lowell. Lowell accepted this without any pettiness and led the negotiations to establish what came to be called the Society of Fellows.

Then there was the question of finances. Sources of large funds were approached, particularly the Rockefeller Foundation, but only polite refusals resulted. Not long after this situation became known, it was announced that an anonymous donor had provided the funds. For a time the anonymity of the donor was absolute, and as long as Mr. Lowell lived it was never admitted in his presence that the source of the funds was known. But when his back was turned, Mr. Whitehead remarked, "Of course, we do not know where the money came from, but we are very glad to have that portrait of Mr. Lowell in our dining room." Mr. Lowell left the note, "In a kind of desperation, I gave it all myself." It represented almost his entire fortune.

The Society of Fellows became a reality in 1933, coinciding with Mr. Lowell's retirement from the Presidency of Harvard. After 30 years, its organization continues almost unchanged. It is worth noting that the Society is responsible only to the President and Fellows of Harvard, not to the Graduate School or to any dean or provost. The structure of the Society is succinctly stated in its formal brochure, from which I quote:

> Ten Senior Fellows, including the President of the University and the Dean of the Faculty of Arts and Sciences, ex officio, administer the Society. The Senior Fellows nominate the Junior

Fellows, meet with them weekly at dinner during term-time, and act as their advisers. Visiting scholars and others come to these dinners as guests and join in the discussions, which are completely informal, and with no set program. In this way the Junior Fellows have an opportunity to meet and talk things over with men of widely different experience and training.

The number of Junior Fellows at any one time is limited to twenty-four, and six to nine have usually been chosen each year. The term of appointment is for three years. At the end of that time a Junior Fellow who has made marked progress toward substantial results may on the recommendation of the Senior Fellows be reappointed for a term not exceeding three years. A candidate for a Junior Fellowship may not have passed his twenty-eighth birthday on July first of the year in which his tenure of the fellowship would begin. In general candidates over twenty-five years of age at the time of their initial appointment may not expect a further appointment beyond their three-year term. . . .

Men interested in any and all fields of study are accepted. They are ordinarily college graduates, and many already have their doctoral degrees. Men who are just taking or have just taken their bachelor's degree are not excluded from consideration, but in general candidates who have completed most of their routine training for advanced work are preferred. During the term of their appointment they are not subject to examination, are not required to make reports, receive no credit for courses, and may not be candidates for any degree, except, however, that candidates for the Ph.D. who have satisfied the preliminary requirements, at Harvard or elsewhere, may proceed to the writing of their theses and to such final or special examination as the university of their candidacy may require, and may be granted the degree of Ph.D. . . .

The unmarried Junior Fellows live in one or another of the Harvard Houses, not in a group, as at the Fondation Thiers. The corporate life of the Society depends on the dinners each Monday night and on weekly luncheons of the Junior Fellows alone. The atmosphere on these occasions is that of a dinner party at home; in fact, any suggestion of ritual is abhorred. There is no certificate or diploma issued. The only token of his tenure which a Junior Fellow acquires is a silver candlestick, added to those on the dining table when he enters and given to him when he leaves.

The Senior Fellows attend the Monday night dinners with commendable loyalty. They have carried out the intention of the founders in devoting an evening a week to serious conversation, but not "shop-talk," with their juniors on an equal footing. To find ten such men, a university must have a large and strong faculty and, even so, they will be found in many different departments and disciplines. At present, there is an economist, a Nobel prize winner in physics, a historian, two experts in comparative literature, a mathematical philosopher, and so on. This makes for a richness of experience and range of contact, which is one of the prime virtues of the Society.

Diversity of interest and expertise among the Senior Fellows is essential in another respect, for to them falls the crucial task of selecting the new Junior Fellows each year. By so doing, they determine the shape and scope of the Society. How are they to go about it? The formal statement is: "Junior Fellows are selected for their resourcefulness, initiative, intellectual curiosity, and promise of notable contribution to one or more of the various fields of knowledge and thought."

Now this is all very well as a generalization, but it is far from simple to apply to individual cases. Since applications are not received and only recommendations from recognized authorities are considered, each is worthy of study, and there are as many as one hundred for a given Junior Fellowship. This situation would be difficult enough if the Senior Fellows had to select one of a hundred historians or one of a hundred physicists or one of a hundred poets. But the difficulties are compounded astronomically when they must select one not only from any one of these fields but of nearly all the others of the arts and sciences. Behind-the-scenes power politics is not unknown, for a Junior Fellowship in a department has become a status symbol of considerable importance. This approach, to the great credit of the Senior Fellows, has been unavailing.

Since the particular man would not be under consideration unless someone of stature had already considered him worthy, letters of recommendation are likely to be so uniformly laudatory as to be useless. Great reliance is placed on the personal interview of the candidate, an interesting observation at the present time when this technique is being derided in most educational circles. But the value of the personal interview depends as much on the skill of the interviewer as on the quality of the man interviewed. At this art, Mr. Henderson and Mr. Whitehead were masters, and they left an example and tradition for their successors. Their aim was at once to place the candidate in as exposed a position as possible.

My own interview might be cited as an example of the technique. Mr. Henderson, whose Tattershall vest and red beard streaked with gray belied his kind heart, presided over a group which included not only Mr. Whitehead, Mr. Lowell, and Mr. Lowes but also George Birkoff, the mathematician, Samuel Eliot Morison, the historian, and others. He began, "This is not an examination, for there is no one in this room competent to examine you." Looking round, I wondered exactly what group he would consider worthy of that task. Then he continued, "All we want to do is to get to know you, and the best way to do that is to talk. So just talk." I will not deny that a perceptible pause followed, for it is easier to talk when there is something to talk about.

The greatest opportunity and deepest obligation imposed by the financial and administrative independence of the Society is boldness in selection of new Junior Fellows. It can afford — it must — choose some men who wish to attack large problems by untried approaches and who may make great success or who may prove dismal failures. Mr. Whitehead pointed out that the excellence of the Prize Fellows of Trinity was maintained because the selecting committee was willing to have as much as 50 per cent failures. As he remarked,

> One day, when I was a member of the Committee, we were faced with two candidates for one fellowship. One was a classicist, who had taken a small problem in Roman history and done it so well that nothing more could be added. The problem was solved and no more work had to be done. The other was a physicist, who presented us with a thesis, of which none of us and none of those we consulted could make head or tail. I went very far in urging the selection of the physicist. Twenty-five years later, I was interested to find out what happened to these two men. The classicist, whom we turned down, was a classics master in a not very important English public school. The physicist, whom we chose, was Eddington.

The opportunity to take such chances in selection is to some extent denied more conventional governing bodies for graduate education, for a series of failures is not likely to be compensated in the eyes of the university administration by a few unexpected successes. One might think this even more true when the support comes from a governmental agency, but my own contacts with this form of educational endeavor suggest that boldness in assuming risk for possible striking gain is more often seen than might have been predicted.

There is one other factor with which the Senior Fellows must deal. Their selections are not a matter of electing the man who strikes them as ablest but one who is able to go from their own field into neighboring fields and, as Mr. Whitehead put it, "shows more evidence of cerebrating than thinking." He it was who defined education as "the acquisition of the art of the utilization of knowledge." It is no kindness to select a man if he would do better to sit down to his job and get on with it. Or, as Mr. Henderson said, "We are not interested in isolated geniuses but in those who do the work of the world."

Now how has all this proved in practice? The Society is just 30 years old this year. In 1958, when it was 25, it was noted that of 148 Junior Fellows, the oldest of whom was in his early fifties and including those who had just finished their terms, 57 held full professorships and 20 associate professorships. One is a Nobel Laureate in physics and three have received Pulitzer Prizes in history and poetry. The report notes that 16 per cent are not in academic life in the strict sense, but I note such activities among these as Director of International Training and Research for the Ford Foundation and Director of the Munson-Williams-Proctor Institute of Art. It seems more than likely that such men have made at least as good use of the Junior Fellowships as some of those in teaching positions.

Mr. Lowell was concerned — even sensitive — about one criticism which was leveled against him and the Society from many sources in its early days: that it encouraged what he called "preciosity," that is, the development of isolated scholars who would contribute nothing to the total academic environment, to say nothing of the world outside. His confidence that this would not be so has been justified by the large number of former Junior Fellows who are heads of departments and by the fact that three have been deans at Harvard alone.

But Mr. Lowell's faith has had another, and perhaps unexpected, form of support from those former Junior Fellows who have participated actively in national and international affairs. One of the first of these was James Fiske, who has interrupted a brilliant career as a nuclear physicist and administrator to serve at Geneva as Chairman of the Western Delegation on detecting violations of nuclear test agreements and on President Eisenhower's Science Advisory Committee in Washington.

More striking is the relation of the Society of Fellows to the Kennedy Administration. It has been said that President Kennedy preferred to depend on generalists rather than narrow specialists for his closest advisors and that he was most successful when he did so. Mr. Kennedy came in more or less contact with many Junior Fellows when he was an undergraduate at Harvard, and he remembered them when he was elected to high office. The most publicized advisors from that source were his special assistants, McGeorge Bundy and Arthur Meier Schlesinger, Jr., but Paul Samuelson played an important role in his policies as advisor in economics. This is not exactly a retreat into the Ivory Tower.

These contributions to responsible public service call to mind the question of whether the structure of the Society may not be especially adapted to the development of such rare and desirable individuals in public life. Certainly the common rooms of English colleges, on which it was largely modeled, have produced British statesmen in numbers for several centuries. But it may be the man and not the environment, for the same individual cannot be trained in more than one way.

And yet the Society of Fellows remains unknown to the general public concerned with education and is not widely recognized beyond restricted academic circles. This is in part due to its fear of publicity, which is in turn the outcome of its cherished formlessness and freedom. A more important part is contributed by the fact that its representatives are spread over most of the fields of knowledge and thought, in which they can be identified only by consulting curricula vitae. Certainly no institution is worse studied in percentages and by other conventional yardsticks.

Perhaps it is all a waste of time and each of the Junior Fellows might have developed in the same way without it. It has done nothing to break the stranglehold of the Ph.D. as a prerequisite for academic positions and has even bowed before this idol to the extent that work done as Junior Fellow may be used for a thesis. To crush the Ph.D. in this regard was one of Mr. Lowell's prime objectives and in it he failed.

The Society of Fellows has had no literal descendants in the establishment of full-scale organizations based on it at other universities, though Yale and the University of Wisconsin each have groups which derive in part from it. The Society has attracted no funds beyond the original gift. This was more than adequate for all its needs at the start, but something has happened to the dollar since 1933. More funds could be used, but the need is not yet acute. More important is that its quite striking results are either unknown or fail to rouse sources of endowment funds, which still exist in some quarters.

Educational experiments of this importance and daring are not numerous. The Society of Fellows has made a notable contribution, all the more so because it depends on people rather than regulations. It is one of the vital strongholds of individualism in a conforming society and thus is doubly precious.

I end on a solemn note, and a confession. There is one bit of ritual in the Society of Fellows. When new members make their first formal appearance at a dinner, a charge is read to them, by Mr. Lowell as long as he lived and by the Chairman after his death. Do not consider this in my prosaic reading. Picture a beautifully proportioned Neo-Georgian room, with eighteenth-century portraits by Smibert and Copley gleaming softly against dark oak panelling in the golden light of a late New England September afternoon. At the center stands Mr. Lowell, a vigorous figure despite his years and honors. Before him, the new Junior Fellows are grouped, each a little bewildered and so new to his task that he has not yet found the concierge. Mr. Lowell's left hand rests gently on the Autocrat of the Breakfast Table's breakfast table; from a paper in his right, he reads, in the most beautiful speaking voice I have ever heard, the noblest call to the life of a scholar known to me:

> You have been selected as a member of this Society for your personal prospect of serious achievement in your chosen field, and your promise of notable contribution to knowledge and thought. That promise you must redeem with your whole intellectual and moral force.
>
> You will practice the virtues, and avoid the snares, of the

scholar. You will be courteous to your elders who have explored to the point from which you may advance; and helpful to your juniors who will progress farther by reason of your labors. Your aim will be knowledge and wisdom, not the reflected glamour of fame. You will not accept credit that is due to another, or harbor jealousy of an explorer who is more fortunate.

You will seek not a near, but a distant, objective, and you will not be satisfied with what you may have done. All that you may achieve or discover you will regard as a fragment of a larger pattern, which from his separate approach every true scholar is striving to descry.

To these things, in joining the Society of Fellows, you dedicate yourself.

CHAPTER NINE

Architecture, Scholarship, Light, and Sherry

IN 1933 A NOBLE EXPERIMENT in education was launched in Cambridge, Massachusetts: The Harvard Society of Fellows. It is our aim here to view this extraordinary manifestation of academic freedom against the backdrop of the university's architecture as it has developed over the centuries, concluding with some personal reminiscences about the early days of the Society and some insights into the thinking and attitudes of its founders. Orville Bailey was appointed to the Society in 1937, and his comments, sixty years later, bear the stamp of personal experience and presence. He wrote about the Society previously in the book, *The Society of Fellows*, with George C. Homans (1948) and in a paper read before the Chicago Literary Club in 1964, "Ask the Concierge," which is Chapter 8 of this volume. David Vopatek's observations are made from an outside and contemporary perspective, enhanced by the opportunity of collaborating with a member whose mentors were central to a time of great innovation and change.

Presented at the Chicago Literary Club by Orville T. Bailey and David R. Vopatek on October 13, 1997, and edited for publication in this volume.

ARCHITECTURE AND SCHOLARSHIP

Harvard's historic but lively setting is inviting and easy to feel at home in. It is, in general, *not* a place of assertive architectural masterpieces, rigid formal planning, or self-contained aloofness that ignores the community outside. Each building, while compatible with the others, is distinctive and stands alone. Indeed, this is the American way. Such independence contrasts with the traditional European manner of subordinating collegiate structures to a harmonious ensemble through such architectural devices as connecting wings, archways, or cloisters. At Harvard the yards, the buildings, and the interiors seem to just whimsically happen and interact as if they had grown naturally, with tales to tell, in a place where a favorite story is always at hand.

Just as Boston is said to be the Athens of America, surely Harvard is its figurative Acropolis, for which the distinctive Society of Fellows would be a suitable Parthenon. In such a place, attitudes influence how things are perceived and over time create lasting feelings and views that often determine how people want their buildings to look. This conditioning, however, with its resulting sense of continuity, is often underestimated. Architects — who converse with God more directly than any Boston Brahmin — may wish to ignore this background and simply decree the current design theology, but anecdotes, memories, and feelings play a role in the school's architectural story as well as in its social chronicles. Fortunately, when traditional styles prompted by such conditioning were applied to Harvard's pre-World War II structures, the work was usually done with a sincerity and depth hard to find in today's more cynical and cost-conscious age.

A building's ability to sustain its character through the Boston

A view of Harvard Yard.

area's many layers of history may differ from that of buildings in other parts of the country where historic structures are closer in time to their origin and original use. Harvard so pre-dates the Revolution that it may seem strange to a Midwesterner, as we approach the end of this century, to learn that the university has spent forty-percent of its existence under the British flag. Indeed, more than half of its life occurred before Chicago was officially born.

Despite their age or design, however, the buildings and communities of Cambridge and Boston have a sense of architectural continuity. Nowhere is this sense of continuity, both in time and place, better illustrated than the view of Harvard's original seven River Houses from Boston, across the Charles River. The seemingly old living quarters with the striking towers of Dunster, Lowell, and Eliot Houses are probably the most photographed and cherished views of the school — for many people, the epitome of how an American college should look. Appearing as if there forever but actually built in the early 1930s, their architectural style can perhaps best be described as Eternal Mock Georgian. They were built during the administration of Abbott Lawrence Lowell, who became president of Harvard in 1909. He succeeded Charles William Eliot, the first of a century of great Harvard presidents following a period of mid-nineteenth-century mediocrity.

Before the houses were built, the area along the Charles was a rundown district of modest homes, commercial use, and mudflats in which the tide of the river ebbed and flowed. It wasn't until a dam was completed downstream in 1910 and a special fund was used to buy the district's numerous small land parcels that it became feasible to clean up the area for something more than sports activities and invite the river to become an integral part of the Harvard landscape. Funds for building came from Edward Stephen Harkness, an alumnus of Yale University. He had offered his alma mater money to build affordable housing in small groups of units thereby making them more humane and manageable, rather than have it construct the usual large and drab institutional–style dormitories. Yale vacillated and could not reach a decision within the time he set, so an irritated Harkness offered the funds to Harvard. Lowell shared his view of housing methods and promptly accepted the money.

While Eliot extended the school's dimensions to north of Harvard Yard beyond Kirkland Street, he remained indifferent to going south of the Yard, where Lowell would triumph with the extensive

River Houses. The one named for Eliot would house the elegant reception and dining rooms for what would become the home of Harvard's most rare and free group of young scholars, The Society of Fellows.

The Society of Fellows' purpose is similar to that of an association of scholars in the Middle Ages, before freedom of study was impaired by degree requirements. Junior Fellows can use any of the university's facilities and courses to investigate whatever sparks their interest. One cannot apply but must be recommended to the Society. Each year new Junior Fellows are selected from all over the world for a three-year term. They must be at the early stage of their careers, so as to be open to discovery, before the risk of their interests and habits solidifying. The Society interviews candidates at its offices a few blocks from Eliot House at 78 Mount Auburn Street. The offices are in a charming frame house, part of which predates the Revolution. There are thirteen Senior Fellows, in addition to the president of the university and the dean of the faculty of Arts and Sciences.

The respect for and the faith placed in Junior Fellows, as well as their opportunity to actually *feel* intellectual freedom, is considered sufficient motivation. Junior Fellows can use all of their time for scholarship, as they are given a large stipend and all of their university fees are paid by the Society. The main idea is to give them support and distinction and treat them as working scholars rather than as students. This provision may have grown out of Lowell's profound fear of faculty members intellectually programming graduate students and using them as a conduit to further their own work, as well as for cheap labor. In a little book called *What a University President Has Learned,* published after he retired, Lowell said, "Where shall wisdom be found and where is the place of understanding?

Offices of the Harvard Society of Fellows at 78 Mt. Auburn Street.

Surely it should be where the pressure of interest is lowest, where men are most free to think and write their own thoughts. . . ."

Monday night dinners are held during term in the Society's rooms at Eliot House. As there is never a formal program, ideas can be freely exchanged with other Junior Fellows, with the Senior Fellows (who treat the former as equals), and with invited guests. Except for the fact that no papers are read, these gatherings are

Entrance to Eliot House, where the Society of Fellows meets.

remarkably similar to those of the Chicago Literary Club. There are also two informal lunch meetings each week in the same rooms without the Senior Fellows, to allow Junior Fellows to converse uninhibited by the weight and judgment of age. When they leave, they are honored not with a certificate but with a silver candlestick from the dining table, as a symbol of light shining from their discoveries.

Lowell's elder kinsman, poet and diplomat James Russell Lowell, referred to a model for the Society in an Alumni Day oration in 1886 when he remarked:

> ... when Cardinal Wolsey built Christ Church at Oxford, his first care was the kitchen. Nothing is so great a quickener of the faculties, or so likely to prevent their being narrowed to a single groove, as the frequent social commingling of men who are aiming at one goal by different paths.... I have often been struck with the many-sided versatility of the Fellows of English colleges who have kept their wits in training by continual fence one with another.

In 1913 a dinner was arranged for the younger Lowell at the Fondation Thiers in Paris, which had fellowships for independent, or what he would later called "productive" scholarship. This experience, along with his knowledge of the Prize Fellows at Trinity College in Cambridge, England, influenced how the Society of Fellows finally evolved under his direction. He noted in his report of 1914–1915: "The holders of such fellowships ought not to be members of any school, because the atmosphere of a school is essentially that of study, and the atmosphere of study is *not* the same as that of production...." He expressed his fear that too much deference went to courses and degrees when he said, "No one should be admitted to candidacy for a doctorate until he is qualified to pursue his education by his own efforts. Courses there should be in the sense of scholars' contributions to knowledge, but neither attendance on them nor examination thereon should be required, and the idea of credit for courses should be left as far behind as supervised study in a school room."

In 1926 productive scholarship was emphasized in "The Report of the Committee of Four" sent to Lowell by Lawrence Joseph Henderson, Charles Pelham Curtis, Jr., John Livingston Lowes, and Alfred North Whitehead. The report basically agreed with Lowell's idea of unimpeded scholarship and fine-tuned the way they felt the future Society of Fellows should be conducted. They, like Lowell, apparently thought that the master's and doctor's degrees had substantially stagnated, becoming little more than certificates indicating the ability to teach (a situation obviously no longer existing today). The report states: "On the whole, contacts between professors and graduate students are in the line of business. Presently the graduates of the colleges and the young Ph.D.'s become parents and teachers, and the vicious circle is complete." Lowell was fond of referring to one dissertation entitled, "The Antennae of the Paleozoic Cockroach." Whitehead always stressed the need for taking a chance on a nominee. When interviewing a candidate, he was more interested in the creative person with room to grow than the one with all the right answers or the perfect paper to which nothing could be added.

Lowell's interest in the Society never waned. Money from donors was not forthcoming, so he gave most of what was left of his own in memory of his wife, Anna Parker Lowell, and set aside rooms for the Society while building Eliot House. He became a Senior Fellow six months after his retirement from the presidency in

November of 1932 and remained active in the Society until his death in January of 1943. Even in retirement he rarely missed a chance to promote Cardinal Wolsey's idea of the value of a kitchen and continual fence with one's fellows. James Russell Lowell would have been proud.

The Society of Fellows, however, was not for Lowell a matter of his final academic cause but fulfillment of what he so passionately worked for, as well as a reflection of his own life. He did his undergraduate work at Harvard and then attended the law school, where he spent two years and took credit for the third by examination. He never received a master's or doctor's degree in the ordinary sense of those terms. When he wrote his various essays and books, including his famous *The Government of England,* he wrote them as a lone scholar.

In addition to his being the right person for his time, Abbott Lawrence Lowell as Harvard's president was able to take advantage of the era's rapid economic expansion to obtain funds for his programs, additional faculty, and new buildings. He was also able to build upon the work of Eliot, who by the end of the nineteenth century had transformed Harvard from a financially wanting college serving primarily New England and New York into the premier national university, as well as a noted international institution. Considering these conditions, it would be hard to imagine formation of the Society of Fellows before Eliot and Lowell. One reason for their great success, in addition to having been on the faculty, was that both men had the means to take a considerable amount of time to do their own research and to reflect, somewhat in the manner of a Junior Fellow, on the direction in which they would like the university to go and how it should be run before ever becoming president.

Harvard President Abbott Lawrence Lowell, a founder and Senior Fellow of the Society of Fellows. (From the files of the Harvard Society of Fellows.)

Lowell's administration complemented Eliot's in many ways, including bringing the undergraduate college, which was lagging, into line with the graduate and professional schools and building much-needed housing. Eliot had emphasized the graduate schools to the detriment of the undergraduate program, and he thought that housing issues should be left to the private sector and the clubs in what was referred to as the "Gold Coast." Lowell gave focus to Eliot's floundering undergraduate elective course system through what he called "concentration and distribution," now known as majors, minors, and electives. He also was concerned that housing based on social cliques or connections would hurt school spirit as well as keep students from learning social skills. Today, largely because of Lowell, Harvard is more egalitarian in its living arrangements than many state schools. It is ironic that such a major effort against the school's social caste system was led by the ultimate Boston Brahmin — Back Bay's quintessential Marlborough Street man.

The general attitude had also changed from the day when Henry Dunster, the college's first president, carried out such great deeds as writing the school's constitution and having its degrees recognized by England's Cambridge and Oxford, only to be edged out when he broke the Puritan law of Massachusetts by questioning infant baptism. Three centuries later, the Unitarian world of Eliot and Lowell was much more open-minded. Perhaps their ties to Kings Chapel and an adjacent burial ground on Boston's Freedom Trail could be a metaphor for Harvard. Here modern liberal Unitarians meet in a stately, understated structure, built by their tradition-minded Episcopalian forefathers, looking over the graves of Puritans.

Harvard can be said to have had five significant periods of building. The first was the medieval seventeenth century. None of the structures from that era remains. The next would be the colonial

Early eighteenth-century housing at Harvard.

and federal years of the eighteenth century and the first two-thirds of the nineteenth. In the eclectic third period, as the twentieth century approached, Eliot would construct as much as his predecessors. In the fourth period, during the first third of the twentieth century, however, Lowell would prove to be Harvard's Augustus. During the twenty years of his administration, he built more than all before him, including using his own money for a lecture hall and a house for the president. James Bryant Conant, who followed Lowell, would bring a new era of science to Harvard but not much building, as he

189

had an economic depression and some war problems to live through. The fifth period would have to wait until Nathan Pusey took over in mid-twentieth century; he oversaw the modern structures and high-rise buildings of a vastly different architecture at Harvard. The funds, mindset, land, and craftsmanship that produced buildings such as the low-rise River Houses no longer existed. One wonders what kind of atmosphere would exist in the rooms that The Society of Fellows occupy had they not been built before the reductive character of architecture's modern movement took hold and had the candles in their silver holders been destined to throw their light upon the sharp edges of steel and glass rather than upon warm wood paneling.

Whatever the current architectural style, however, the university has a record of producing the best buildings it could for their time. The early seventeenth-century structures did not last because their methods of construction could not cope with a new and harsher climate. It was not until Massachusetts Hall, the Yard's oldest surviving structure, was begun in 1719 in Early Georgian style that Harvard's architecture would be in for a change. The new buildings would now be better built, have more design cohesion, and would not have to be self-contained for all functions, from living to teaching. It was not until the 1880s, however, that sanitation and heating problems would be adequately, although primitively, addressed with plumbing and central heating, a development contributing to the configuration of the Yard as it is today. Electricity was introduced in 1891, which allowed the main library, then in the Gothic-style Gore Hall (now demolished), to be used at night. Gas and candles were not allowed to throw light upon knowledge because the building was not fireproof. That kind of facility would have to wait until construction of the Widener Library in 1913.

Dunster House, one of the original seven River Houses built during the adminis-tration of Abbott Lawrence Lowell.

There were a number of examples and proposals for planning new buildings, such as The Harvard Overseers Plan of 1896, which depicted a grand boulevard from the Yard to the Charles River where the River Houses stand today, as well as a formal axial layout of the Medical School. But all of this rigid grandeur was rejected by Lowell who, as virtually the university's sole link with the Corporation and the Overseers, Harvard's two governing bodies, was in a position to make the major decisions — which he did. Eliot was not much interested in such matters, despite having a son who was a landscape architect. Lowell, however, fancied himself an amateur architect, loved to go over plans, and enjoyed prowling through construction sites in off hours with his dog. While he had a very good relationship with Charles A. Coolidge, who would plan the River Houses, their design — including scale, style, and room layout — was Lowell's choice. The houses are divided into groups of rooms around a central study with a fireplace. Each group has its own entrance, rather than a system of forbidding, institutional-looking corridors. Lowell wanted the rooms designed so that a group living together would be small enough for one to feel at home but large enough to allow one to escape cliques.

The same approach would govern the size of the Society of Fellows. There is, of course, no absolute method to prove the optimal size for the Society or for the student living quarters in the River Houses, except to say that their exemplary results speak for themselves. Lowell, like Eliot, knew what he wanted, and he had a way of taking seemingly unrelated forces and pulling them together at the right time, as if grabbing stray light beams and focussing them to shine on his goals.

Some observers will question this explanation, attributing the outcomes to the force of strong personalities working against propi-

The dining table set for a Society dinner.

tious events rather than seeing them as complementing each other. Others will foolishly ponder history's eternal question: *What if?* What would be the format for the Society's meetings if Lowell had not been familiar with Cardinal Wolsey's kitchen or if he had not had dinner in Paris at the Fondation Thiers? What if he had not brought White-head to Cambridge from the English version of Harvard or if Lowes had gone off to some Xanadu? What if Yale had ceased its foolish procrastination and accepted all of the Harkness money in a timely way instead of forfeiting a large part of it to Harvard to build the

Orville Bailey in conversation with Diana Morse.

River Houses? Would the university be its present size if the water level in the Charles, or for that matter the privies in the Yard, could not have been controlled? Indeed, would the Philosophy Department save Harvard if the Day of Judgment came and the Puritans rose up and drove the heathen Unitarians out of Kings Chapel and then staged a demonstration in Harvard Yard, demanding their college back?!

The Society's dignified exterior entrance is discreetly located in a low wing off the main body of Eliot House near the end of a quiet side street. Inside, the elegant reception and dining rooms resemble the first floor of a Georgian row house and overlook a lawn and the

Master's garden. There is also a kitchen, pantry, and washroom. The rooms are furnished with an interesting mix of memorabilia extending back through the Society's history. For example, sherry, which always precedes dinner, is served from the table used by Oliver Wendell Holmes — that is, the Autocrat of the Breakfast Table's breakfast table. The U-shaped dining table was made for that room and is set with the special candlesticks that have always been the emblem of the Society. There are thoughtfully placed pictures of thoughtful faces looking down from majestic paneled walls, and a plaque of Lowell affirms the room as a place where *veritas* reigns.

Indeed, one can imagine Lowell making his introductory statement to new Junior Fellows, in which he admonishes, "All that you may achieve or discover you will regard as a fragment of a larger pattern, which from his separate approach every true scholar is striving to descry." His reference to fragments of a larger pattern is, in a sense, reflected in the eclectic nature of the furnishings in the Society's rooms and the derivative Georgian-style building housing them, as well as in the overall serendipitous setting of the university itself. It is also a reminder that Harvard's architecture and scholarship differ from its earlier medieval and classical heritage. Now the buildings and the learning that takes place within them are no longer self-contained entities but are open-ended in a much larger world. This freedom, indeed, is the theme of the Society and is evident in the ambience of its rooms, even as it is juxtaposed with the continuity of the building's Georgian style.

LIGHT AND SHERRY

Although Society lunches are casual, dinner is a formal affair. When Orville Bailey and David Vopatek arrived for dinner one evening in May 1997, they were given a gracious welcome by Diana Morse, who oversees the Society's day-to-day affairs, and its chairman, Nobel Laureate Walter Gilbert. The atmosphere in the reception room was both jovial and interesting, and everyone seemed eager to share her and his thoughts. In other words, the noble experiment was working. Willard Van Orman Quine, who once filled Whitehead's role at Harvard, made a point of coming that evening to see Orville Bailey. And, in a coincidence that made the guests feel even more at home, several people were talking about Chicago, including Junior Fellows Sudhir Venkatesh, a sociologist from the University of Chicago who had written about the city's urban affairs, and Steven Levitt, an economist who was about to assume a teaching post at the University of Chicago.

All of a sudden, as in the grand finale of an opera, all the elements of a memorable evening came together. The beaming faces of the Fellows and Bailey's proud smile of homecoming announced its success, and the rich luster of the wood paneled walls nurtured it. Meanwhile, the dining room was being prepared in a manner that would have made Cardinal Wolsey happy. Bottles of fine wine were uncorked as the table was set, the candles in the silver candlesticks were lit, and the heavy curtains were drawn just as the clock struck six. It was time for sherry.

The foregoing pages represent an attempt to describe the Society of Fellows in the context of an emerging Harvard. But sherry brings a time for personal reflection. The following comments by

Sherry time — an extension of Cardinal Wolsey's kitchen.

Orville Bailey reach back more than half a century to the early days of the Society and to the men who shaped and breathed life into it, touching on the essence of the silver candlestick.

* * *

In these quiet and gracious rooms, two groups of scholars have assembled each Monday evening for dinner in term time since September 25, 1933, at half past six. One group is made up of the Senior Fellows, master scholars well along in their intellectual careers, and the other of carefully chosen young people, beginning careers of their own. The purpose of the meeting is good conversation in an atmosphere of academic freedom.

In my day, from 1937 to 1940, pride of place went to Abbott Lawrence Lowell. He had retired from a long career as president of the university, but his earlier achievements were in the field of constitutional law, especially the unwritten English Constitution. In this regard, there is a peculiar contradiction which has often been pointed out: As an American Mr. Lowell knew more about the English constitution than anyone else, while Lord Gray knew more about the American constitution than any American. Mr. Lowell's term as president of Harvard saw much building construction and both the quantitative and qualitative enhancement of faculty, including the first Nobel Prize to come to a member of the Harvard faculty. As he reached old age, he became increasingly concerned about the rigidity of the requirements of the Ph.D. degree at a time when young scholars are working their way to major achievement.

Despite the fact that Mr. Lowell had made the Society of Fellows possible by endowing it with his large fortune, it was Lawrence Joseph Henderson who was named chairman and did the basic work that gave the Society form and substance. Henderson was a man of

Orville Bailey with a portrait of L.J. Henderson.

Lawrence Joseph Henderson, a founder and the first chairman of the Society.
(From the files of the Harvard Society of Fellows.)

unusually varied talents. By profession he was a biochemist who had made the great contribution of applying physical chemistry to biological systems, but this was only the beginning of his talents. He taught not only a course in biochemistry but also one in the history of science, as well as two more in sociology. It has been said that he could teach a better course in the modern French novel than anyone in the romance Language Department had he chosen to do so.

Henderson was also a brilliant and urbane conversationalist. One of his remarks I have treasured for over half a century: "The secret of human happiness is not being concerned about things which you can do nothing about." Of music, he had only the attitude expected in modern intellectuals. One evening he remarked, "I soon tire of Wagner, I eventually tire of Beethoven, but Mozart seems to have a direct pipeline to the source of inspiration." It is often said, and it is quite possible, that it was he who selected the candlestick as the only symbol of membership in the Society. Certainly it is true that he selected the mold from which the candlesticks were made. He told about searching the antique shops of Eastern Europe and finding at last a brass one which was deemed suitable and was copied in silver.

One of the most splendid of Burgundy wines is Chambertin. The area producing it is small and surrounded by a wide area of lesser wine production called Gevre Chambertin, which is much less expensive than that of the grand central area. L.J. Henderson was looking for a good but reasonably priced wine for the Society. He commented:

> I spent the summer of 1934 in Europe. I had a friend who owned a strip of vines just over the fence from Chambertin. Now, soils don't change so rapidly, but his wine, by French law,

could only be sold as Gevre Chambertin. I tasted and tasted, and at the end of the summer I bought enough of it to last the Society ten years — and for me for the rest of my life-time.

The wine was pronounced mediocre by the authorities of that period, but later they came to list it as one of the great vintages of the century. The genial housekeeper of the Society saw how much I liked that wine and served it whenever I was there. When war came shortly after that, Mr. Henderson urged former Junior Fellows who were doing work in the Harvard area to come as often as they could to keep the young Society going. This I did, so I was able to follow the wine from the days when it was too young, to its glorious maturity, and on until it began to fade in the mid-forties. It fully justified Henderson's claim to be a wine connoisseur, and I was only one of the beneficiaries of his skill.

Henderson was joined in selecting Junior Fellows by Alfred North Whitehead, who had helped to choose the Prize Fellows of Trinity College in Cambridge, England. The English school had much to do with its American counterpart in form. Attracting Mr. Whitehead to Harvard was one of Mr. Lowell's greatest triumphs as president. Commonly regarded as having one of he finest minds of the twentieth century, Whitehead was known for his great work *Principia Mathematica*. He was supposedly assisted in his accomplishment by Bertrand Russell, but Russell actually did little more than read the proof. I went to see him frequently. He was a kindly, slightly overweight old man who could dominate any conversation. One day I asked him what he thought of Bertrand Russell. He replied, "Beloved as a dear man and a good mathematical logician, but when he talks about statesmanship, I pay no attention, you know."

Alfred North Whitehead, the author of Principia Mathematica *and a founder of the Society.* (From the files of the Harvard Society of Fellows.)

Mr. Whitehead's constant worry was that in selecting new Junior Fellows the Seniors would take no chances, something he felt was important for them to do. He cited an experience with the Prize Fellows of Trinity, in which two candidates presented theses and it was a question as to which to choose. One was a classicist whose thesis was so complete and well done that it never could have been improved. The other was a physicist, although nobody could make out what he was doing. Whitehead insisted on choosing the physicist, and prevailed. When he followed up on the result 25 years later, the classicist had a routine job in a public school, and the physicist was world famous in his field.

Mr. Whitehead's greatest delight was intellectual conversation on a specific topic. He missed this when he came to New England, and he went about trying to improve matters. It was only one of the reasons for his involvement with the Society of Fellows, but an important one. He supplemented Society meetings by inviting groups of people to his home every Sunday. He and his charming wife carried on intellectual conversation, for Mrs. Whitehead was as good a conversationalist as her husband. She was as thin as he was heavy, and her conversation had even more brilliance than his. There I received much of the material for the history of the Society on which the book entitled, *The Society of Fellows, Harvard University,* is based. These evenings were unforgettable, and I will cherish the memory of them for the rest of my life.

In the early days of the Society, literature was represented by John Livingston Lowes — a brilliant choice. In his famous book, *The Road to Xanadu,* he looks more deeply into the mechanism of creative writing than anyone before or since. Most tragically, by 1937 Lowes was severely affected by Alzheimer's disease, getting lost on the way home and confusing people he knew well. His usefulness, which could have been so great, was almost nil by the time I entered as a Junior Fellow.

There were two ex officio Senior Fellows who attended meetings but took no part in the selection of Junior Fellows. At that time they were George Birkhoff, Dean of Arts and Sciences, and James Bryant Conant, president of the university. With his other duties, Conant could not be expected to come often, but he did come three times during my term and he proved an interesting and brilliant conversationalist. Once a great professor of chemistry, he also became a great administrator.

The first group of Senior Fellows was a remarkable group. They combined the highest eminence of scholarship with skill in stimulating young people. The success of the Society depends on finding both capabilities in the same individual, and Mr. Henderson once expressed concern over whether the two could be found in members of such a small group. Two Senior Fellows were soon added, however, proving his worries unwarranted. One of these was Samuel Eliot Morison, an eminent historian of both naval and American history. When World War II began, he was asked by President Franklin D. Rooosevelt to write a history of its naval operations, viewing these as they occurred. His work was published in a large series of volumes that perhaps made World War II better recorded than any other war. With all this, Morison most appreciated compliments on his early book, *Maritime History of Massachusetts, 1783-1860*. Morison was a kindly person and much appreciated in the Society. He invited me several times to his holiday home on Mount Desert and once to a grand party at his home on Brimmer Street at the foot of Beacon Hill.

The other Senior Fellow added early was Arthur Darby Nock, who was a classicist — perhaps the greatest in the world — and whose

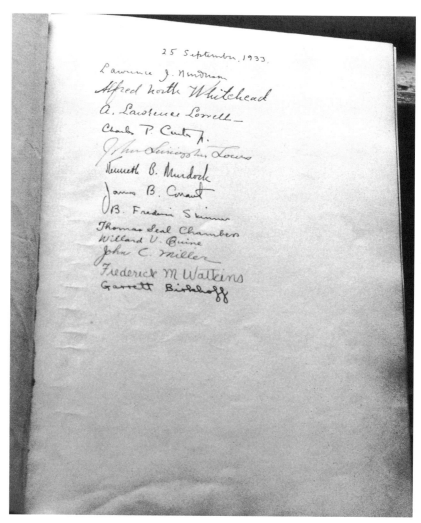

Signatures in the Society guest book, 1933.

Signatures in the Society guest book, 1937.

A gathering of Society members in 1940, with Orville Bailey standing at far right.
(From the files of the Harvard Society of Fellows.)

magnum opus was to be on the Hellenistic religion. Unfortunately, he died before it was completed, but it was prepared for publication by others. He came originally from the English Cambridge, where his absence was greatly felt. A bachelor, he lived in a suite of rooms in Eliot House, where he easily kept an eye on the Society and its rooms. He had ambition to succeed Mr. Henderson as chairman, but the post finally went to another Harvard man.

With such eminent scholars presiding in such splendid architecture, it is fair to ask what the results have been. One criterion might be the nearly dozen Nobel Prizes received, especially impressive considering the small number of Fellows and the fact that many are in fields for which there are no Nobel Prizes. We might, for example, look at the Junior fellows admitted in 1937. There were five available places, plus a few surviving second terms. One of these went to John Bardeen. At that time he was painfully shy, and we wondered how he could live up to the reputation of his father, who had recently had a building named after him at the University of Wisconsin. But he soon did the neater trick of winning the Nobel Prize twice.

At the same time there was a brilliant young chemist named Robert Woodward — so young that it was thought he might well burn out. The Senior Fellows decided to place him for a year with Harvard's leading teacher of chemists to see what would happen. At the end of the year, Henderson asked for an evaluation from the professor and received one which he said was the most valuable he ever received. It consisted of only two sentences: "I had a problem that I had worked on for two years and could not solve. I gave it to Woodward and he solved it in a month." Admission to the Society of Fellows was immediate, and the Nobel Prize was not far off.

When Nobel decided to leave his great fortune for prizes, the social sciences were in rudimentary form, and did not warrant a prize in that area. As time went on, however, the disciplines developed rapidly and the income from the Nobel estate increased even more rapidly. It thus was decided to establish a prize in the social sciences. The first to receive this distinction was a former Junior Fellow, economist Paul Samuelson.

It is also worth noting that much of the glamour of the Kennedy Administration was due to former Junior Fellows whom he invited to join him in Washington. One was later to write the definitive history of the era, Arthur Meier Schlesinger, Jr.

In addition to Nobel Prizes, Society of Fellows members have received Pulitzer Prizes and other honors almost without number. But prizes are not the aim of the Society. Mr. Henderson once remarked to me, "What we want are people who will do the work of the world." He would be pleased to see the heads of departments and leaders in education who were former Junior Fellows now in positions of power not only at Harvard but all across the nation. The white candles glow ever more brightly from ocean to ocean. They burn in many places — a dozen in the Chicago area alone — and they add to the distinction of American academic life. But is this result wholly due to the mixture of architecture, scholarship, and sherry? As so often happens, the final word belongs to Shakespeare:

> *How far that little candle throws his beams!*
> *So shines a good deed in a naughty world.*

BIBLIOGRAPHY

Bunting, Bainbridge, and Margaret Henderson Floyd. *Harvard: An Architectural History.* Cambridge, Mass.: Harvard University Press, 1985.

Greenslet, Ferris: *The Lowells and Their Seven Worlds.* Boston: Houghton Mifflin, 1946.

Homans, George. C., and Orville T. Bailey. *The Society of Fellows, Harvard University.* Cambridge, Mass.: Harvard University, 1948.

Morison, Samuel Eliot. *The Founding of Harvard College.* Cambridge, Mass.: Harvard University Press, 1935.

Morison, Samuel Eliot. *Three Centuries of Harvard.* Cambridge, Mass.: Belnap Press, 1936.

Notes on the Harvard Tercentenary. Cambridge, Mass: Harvard University Press, 1936.

Yomans, Henry Aaron. *Abbott Lawrence Lowell, 1856–1943.* Cambridge, Mass.: Harvard University Press, 1948.

The authors acknowledge the assistance and encouragement of Diana Morse, Administrator of the Society, who also graciously reviewed and commented on the manuscript. Walter Gilbert, Chairman of the Society, and Mary Daniels of the Harvard Library System were supportive and helpful. Constructive criticism was given by Frances Conway of Kenilworth, Illinois; Beatrice Olsen of Kalamazoo, Michigan; and Douglas Olsen of Needham, Massachusetts.

Epilogue

⤳

THROUGHOUT HIS LONG LIFE, Orville T. Bailey retained a great affinity for Boston and Harvard, the locus of his development as a pioneer in the new field of neuropathology and his emergence as a man of the world, at ease in sophisticated society. On his last trip in the spring of 1997, the Boston Public Garden was resplendent with the season's bulbs in full bloom against the backdrop of ancient trees. He basked in its varied beauty, his lifelong love of plants and flowers as strong and gratifying as ever. He visited the Harvard Society of Fellows then, as recounted in Chapter Nine, more than six decades after his appointment to that select group. As it turned out, this homecoming would also be his farewell, prior to his death in 1998. Returning to Boston and Harvard offered him both rejuvenation and comfort. Some things changed there over the years, but for the most part the beautiful old city and the august university just across the river remained faithful constants for him — homeports in a life that traversed this country and the world.

Less frequently he visited his birthplace among the mountain peaks of Greene County, New York, where, contrary to his Boston experience, there was hardly a shred of connection to the past. For years there have been no family members living in Jewett, and

213

Mountain Side House resort and its farm are but memories: The buildings are long gone, no cows graze in the pastures, and silence has replaced the bustle of city people enjoying themselves in the country on sunny summer afternoons. A black asphalt road passes where the main house stood and winds its way up through the old orchard to the steep part of the mountain, scattering putative house lots at its sides. The "fair meadows" of the early part of the twentieth century have been overwhelmed by brush and trees, and even the old logging roads are mostly indistinguishable. In short, the magic has gone from the place.

Just over the shoulder of the mountain is a valley through which flows the Batavia Kill, a meandering stream except in the spring melt or in periods of heavy rain. On a hillside looking across this valley toward the mountain is the cemetery where Orville T. Bailey lies at journey's end with his mother and father. As a boy on his way to school in Windham, he would have passed this place frequently, walking or riding in a horse-drawn conveyance, no doubt preoccupied with thoughts of his current studies or observing the season's offering of flora and fauna.

When he returned here for the last time in October of 1998, a small group of family and friends attended a ceremony in Windham, then gathered at graveside for a final farewell. At the age of 89 he had simply outlived nearly all the contemporaries of his youth. A cousin, Richard Bailey, spoke of Orville Bailey's early days in Jewett and his love of nature and the mountains, and David Vopatek, a devoted friend of many years, read at his longstanding request a poem he had chosen for the occasion. Written by the English poet A.E. Housman, it is entitled, "For My Funeral." Its stark beauty somehow made it most appropriate for the man and the setting, and as the final words in this collection of his writings:

O thou that from thy mansion
  Through time and place to roam,
Dost send abroad thy children,
  And then dost call them home,

That men and tribes and nations
  And all thy hand hath made
May shelter them from sunshine
  In thine eternal shade:

We now to peace and darkness
  And earth and thee restore
Thy creature that thou madest
  And wilt cast forth no more.

E.R.B.

*Orville Bailey's Chicago residence on North Pine Grove Avenue. (*Drawing by David R. Vopatek.*)*